GREAT SERMONS OF THE
TWENTIETH CENTURY

GREAT
SERMONS
of the
TWENTIETH
CENTURY

Compiled by
PETER F. GUNTHER

CROSSWAY BOOKS • WESTCHESTER, ILLINOIS
A DIVISION OF GOOD NEWS PUBLISHERS

Book design by K. L. Mulder

First printing, 1986

Printed in the United States of America

Library of Congress Catalog Card Number 86-70286

ISBN 0-89107-397-3

Table of Contents

Preface   vii

The Waning Authority of Christ in the Churches   9
    A. W. TOZER (1897-1963)

What Will the Lord Say to Us All When He Returns?   17
    WILLIAM CULBERTSON (1905-1971)

If Good Men Will Not . . .   27
    V. RAYMOND EDMAN (1900-1967)

The Christian Message to the World   35
    D. MARTYN LLOYD-JONES (1899-1981)

The Eternal Security of the Believer   49
    HENRY ALLAN IRONSIDE (1878-1951)

Your Right to Heaven   63
    DONALD GREY BARNHOUSE (1895-1960)

The Birthday of Souls   71
    JAMES McGINLAY (1901-1958)

When God's Patience Wears Out!   81
    JOHN R. RICE (1895-1980)

Payday Someday   97
    ROBERT G. LEE (1886-1978)

Other Little Ships   129
    HERBERT LOCKYER, SR. (1886-1984)

Affirming the Will of God   137
    PAUL E. LITTLE (1928-1975)

No Little People, No Little Places   153
    FRANCIS A. SCHAEFFER (1912-1984)

Acknowledgments   165

Preface

The Christian church has been blessed with great preachers throughout history. Sermons by St. Augustine, Martin Luther, John Calvin, John Knox, Jonathan Edwards, John Wesley, George Whitefield, Charles Spurgeon, D. L. Moody, and others have left their imprint on the life of the church.

God has seen fit to continue to give the church great preachers in the twentieth century. Men like R. A. Torrey, Billy Sunday, Wilber Chapman, Gypsy Smith, and Louis T. Talbot have been some of the leaders God has used in the last eighty years in Bible teaching, evangelism, and in the development of great movements.

Sermons in this volume have been selected not so much by the fact that the men were great preachers, but rather on the basis of the impact these particular sermons have had. Many more sermons could have been included. The sermons given here were preached by men whose public ministries have been terminated by death, but whose messages continue to speak to the church today.

A. W. Tozer
1897-1963

A. W. Tozer was one of the most penetrating preachers of his day.
His philosophy was, "Everything is wrong until God sets it right."
He exposed sin and urged people to surrender to Christ. His desire
was to get people to know God in a personal way and to grow to be
like Him.

Tozer pastored Christian and Missionary Alliance churches in
West Virginia, Ohio, and Indiana, as well as in Chicago and
Toronto. However, he no doubt reached more people through his
writing. He was editor of The Alliance Witness, and his editorials
were worth the price of the subscription. He wrote with conviction
and had the gift of making spiritual truths reach the heart.

"The Waning Authority of Christ in the Churches" was published in The Alliance Witness on May 15, 1963, a few days
after his sudden heart attack that ended his ministry. It is available
in tract form through Christian Publications, Inc., 3825 Hartzdale
Drive, Camp Hill, Pennsylvania 17011.

The Waning
Authority
of Christ
in the Churches

Here is the burden of my heart; and while I claim for myself no special inspiration I yet feel that this is also the burden of the Spirit.

If I know my own heart it is love alone that moves me to write this. What I write here is not the sour ferment of a mind agitated by contentions with my fellow Christians. There have been no such contentions. I have not been abused, mistreated, or attacked by anyone. Nor have these observations grown out of any unpleasant experiences that I have had in my association with others. My relations with my own church as well as with Christians of other denominations have been friendly, courteous, and pleasant. My grief is simply the result of a condition which I believe to be almost universally prevalent among the churches.

I think also that I should acknowledge that I am myself very much involved in the situation I here deplore. As Ezra in his mighty prayer of intercession included himself among the wrongdoers, so do I. "O my God, I am ashamed and blush to lift up my face to Thee, my God: for our iniquities are increased over our head, and our trespass is grown up unto the heavens." Any hard word spoken here against others must in simple honesty return upon my own head. I too have been guilty. This is written with the hope that we all may turn unto the Lord our God and sin no more against Him.

Let me state the cause of my burden. It is this: *Jesus Christ has today almost no authority at all among the groups that call themselves*

9

by His name. By these I mean not the Roman Catholics, nor the Liberals, nor the various quasi-Christian cults. I do mean Protestant churches generally, and I include those that protest the loudest that they are in spiritual descent from our Lord and His apostles—namely, the evangelicals.

It is a basic doctrine of the New Testament that after His resurrection, the Man Jesus was declared by God to be both Lord and Christ, and that He was invested by the Father with absolute Lordship over the church which is His body. All authority is His in heaven and in earth. In His own proper time He will exert it to the full, but during this period in history, He allows this authority to be challenged or ignored. And just now it is being challenged by the world and ignored by the church.

The present position of Christ in the gospel churches may be likened to that of a king in a limited, constitutional monarchy. The king (sometimes depersonalized by the term "the Crown") is in such a country no more than a traditional rallying point, a pleasant symbol of unity and loyalty much like a flag or a national anthem. He is lauded, feted, and supported, but his real authority is small. Nominally he is head over all, but in every crisis someone else makes the decisions. On formal occasions he appears in his royal attire to deliver the tame, colorless speech put into his mouth by the real rulers of the country. The whole thing may be no more than good-natured make-believe, but it is rooted in antiquity, it is a lot of fun, and no one wants to give it up.

Among the gospel churches Christ is now in fact little more than a beloved symbol. "All Hail the Power of Jesus' Name" is the church's national anthem and the cross is her official flag, but in the week-by-week services of the church and the day-by-day conduct of her members, someone else, not Christ, makes the decisions. Under proper circumstances Christ is allowed to say, "Come unto me, all ye that labor and are heavily laden" or "Let not your heart be troubled." But when the speech is finished, someone else takes over. Those in actual authority decide the moral standards of the church, as well as all objectives and all methods employed to achieve them. Because of long and meticulous organization, it is now possible for the youngest pastor just out of seminary to have more actual authority in a church than Jesus Christ has.

Not only does Christ have little or no authority; His influence also is becoming less and less. I would not say that He has none, only that it is small and diminishing. A fair parallel would be the influence of Abraham Lincoln over the American people. Honest Abe is still the idol of the country. The likeness of his kind, rugged face, so homely that it is beautiful, appears everywhere. It is easy to grow misty-eyed over him. Children are brought up on stories of his love, his honesty, and his humility. But after we have gotten control over our tender emotions, what have we left? No more than a good example which, as it recedes into the past, becomes more and more unreal and exercises less and less real influence. Every scoundrel is ready to wrap Lincoln's long black coat around him. In the cold light of political facts in the United States, the constant appeal to Lincoln by the politicians is a cynical joke.

The Lordship of Jesus is not quite forgotten among Christians, but it has been mostly relegated to the hymnal where all responsibility toward it may be comfortably discharged in a glow of pleasant religious emotion. Or if it is taught as a theory in the classroom, it is rarely applied to practical living. The idea that the Man Christ Jesus has absolute and final authority over the whole church and over all of its members in every detail of their lives is simply not now accepted as true by the rank and file of evangelical Christians.

What we do is this: We accept the Christianity of our group as being identical with that of Christ and His apostles. The beliefs, the practices, the ethics, the activities of our group are equated with the Christianity of the New Testament. Whatever the group thinks or says or does is Scriptural, no questions asked. It is assumed that all our Lord expects of us is that we busy ourselves with the activities of the group. In so doing we are keeping the commandments of Christ.

To avoid the hard necessity of either obeying or rejecting the plain instructions of our Lord in the New Testament, we take refuge in a liberal interpretation of them. Casuistry is not the possession of Roman Catholic theologians alone. We evangelicals also know how to avoid the sharp point of obedience by means of fine and intricate explanations. These are tailor-made for the flesh. They excuse disobedience, comfort carnality, and make the words of Christ of none effect. And the essence of it all is that Christ simply could not have meant what He said. His teachings are accepted even theoretically only after they have been weakened by interpretation.

11

Yet Christ is consulted by increasing numbers of persons with "problems" and sought after by those who long for peace of mind. He is widely recommended as a kind of spiritual psychiatrist with remarkable powers to straighten them out. He is able to deliver them from their guilt complexes and to help them avoid serious psychic traumas by making a smooth and easy adjustment to society and to their own ids. Of course this strange Christ has no relation whatever to the Christ of the New Testament. The true Christ is also Lord, but this accommodating Christ is little more than the servant of the people.

But I suppose I should offer some concrete proof to support my charge that Christ has little or no authority today among the churches. Well, let me put forward a few questions and let the answers be the evidence.

What church board consults our Lord's words to decide matters under discussion? Let anyone reading this who has had experience on a church board try to recall the times or time when any board member read from the Scriptures to make a point, or when any chairman suggested that the brethren should see what instructions the Lord had for them on a particular question. Board meetings are habitually opened with a formal prayer or "a season of prayer"; after that, the Head of the church is respectfully silent while the real rulers of the church take over. Let anyone who denies this bring forth evidence to refute it. I for one will be glad to hear it.

What Sunday school committee goes to the Word for directions? Do not the members invariably assume that they already know what they are supposed to do and that their only problem is to find effective means to get it done? Plans, rules, "operations," and new methodological techniques absorb all their time and attention. The prayer before the meeting is for divine help to carry out their plans. Apparently the idea that the Lord might have some instructions for them never so much as enters their heads.

Who remembers when a conference chairman brought his Bible to the table with him for the purpose of using it? Minutes, regulations, rules of order, yes. The sacred commandments of the Lord, no. An absolute dichotomy exists between the devotional period and the business session. The first has no relation to the second.

What foreign mission board actually seeks to follow the guidance of the Lord as provided by His Word and His Spirit? They all think they do, but what they do in fact is to assume the Scripturalness of their ends and then ask for help to find ways to achieve them. They may pray all night for God to give success to their enterprises, but Christ is desired as their helper, not as their Lord. Human means are devised to achieve ends assumed to be divine. These harden into policy, and thereafter the Lord doesn't even have a vote.

In the conduct of our public worship, where is the authority of Christ to be found? The truth is that today the Lord rarely controls a service, and the influence He exerts is very small. We sing of Him and preach about Him, but He must not interfere; we worship our way, and it must be right because we have always done it that way, as have the other churches in our group.

What Christian when faced with a moral problem goes straight to the Sermon on the Mount or other New Testament Scripture for the authoritative answer? Who lets the words of Christ be final on giving, birth control, the bringing up of a family, personal habits, tithing, entertainment, buying, selling, and other such important matters?

What theological school, from the lowly Bible institute up, could continue to operate if it were to make Christ Lord of its every policy? There may be some, and I hope there are, but I believe I am right when I say that most such schools, to stay in business, are forced to adopt procedures which find no justification in the Bible they profess to teach. So we have this strange anomaly: the authority of Christ is ignored in order to maintain a school to teach among other things the authority of Christ.

The causes back of the decline in our Lord's authority are many. I name only two.

One is the power of custom, precedent, and tradition within the older religious groups. These, like gravitation, affect every particle of religious practice within the group, exerting a steady and constant pressure in one direction. Of course that direction is toward conformity to the status quo. Not Christ but custom is lord in this situation. And the same thing has passed over (possibly to a slightly lesser degree) into the other groups such as the Full Gospel tabernacles, the holiness churches, the Pentecostal and fundamental churches, and the many independent and undenominational churches found everywhere throughout the North American continent.

The second cause is the revival of intellectualism among the evangelicals. This, if I sense the situation correctly, is not so much a thirst for learning as a desire for a reputation of being learned. Because of it, good men who ought to know better are being put in the position of collaborating with the enemy. I'll explain.

Our evangelical faith (which I believe to be the true faith of Christ and His apostles) is being attacked these days from many different directions. In the Western world the enemy has forsworn violence. He comes against us no more with sword and fagot; he now comes smiling, bearing gifts. He raises his eyes to heaven and swears that he too believes in the faith of our fathers. But his real purpose is to destroy that faith, or at least to modify it to such an extent that it is no longer the supernatural thing it once was. He comes in the name of philosophy or psychology or anthropology, and with sweet reasonableness urges us to rethink our historic position, to be less rigid, more tolerant, more broadly understanding.

He speaks in the sacred jargon of the schools, and many of our half-educated evangelicals run to fawn on him. He tosses academic degrees to the scrambling sons of the prophets as Rockefeller used to toss dimes to the children of the peasants. The evangelicals who, with some justification, have been accused of lacking true scholarship now grab for these status symbols with shining eyes, and when they get them they are scarcely able to believe their eyes. They walk about in a kind of ecstatic unbelief, much as the soloist of the neighborhood church choir might were she to be invited to sing at La Scala.

For the true Christian, the one supreme test for the present soundness and ultimate worth of everything religious must be the place our Lord occupies in it. Is He Lord or symbol? Is He in charge of the project or merely one of the crew? Does He decide things or only help to carry out the plans of others? All religious activities from the simplest act of an individual Christian to the ponderous and expansive operations of a whole denomination may be proved by the answer to the question, Is Jesus Christ Lord in this act? Whether our works prove to be wood, hay, and stubble or gold and silver and precious stones in that great day will depend upon the right answer to that question.

What then are we to do? Each one of us must decide, and there are at least three possible choices. One is to rise up in shocked indignation and accuse me of irresponsible reporting.

14

Another is to nod general agreement with what is written here but take comfort in the fact that there are exceptions and we are among the exceptions. The other is to go down in meek humility and confess that we have grieved the Spirit and dishonored our Lord in failing to give Him the place His Father has given Him as Head and Lord of the church. Either the first or the second will but confirm the wrong. The third, if carried out to its conclusion, can remove the curse. The decision lies with us.

William Culbertson
1905-1971

Dr. William Culbertson was ordained in the Reformed Episcopal Church in 1928. He became a bishop in 1937 and taught at Reformed Episcopal Seminary before becoming lecturer and dean at Moody Bible Institute. He served as president of the Institute from 1948-1971.

Dr. Culbertson was in great demand as a conference speaker, often identified as a "deeper life preacher" and a "pastor's pastor." He traveled frequently to Great Britain to speak at the Keswick conventions as well as in churches throughout the British Isles.

He also had a love for missions and visited mission fields around the world.

In the summer of 1971, Dr. Culbertson ministered again in Great Britain. On September 5 of that same year he spoke at Winona Lake, Indiana on "What Will the Lord Say to Us All When He Returns?" This was his last message. He died in Chicago on November 16, 1971. His final words were, "God—God—Yes!"

What Will the Lord Say to Us All When He Returns?

We have been thinking together about the coming of the Lord for His own, when "the Lord Himself shall descend from heaven, with a shout, with the voice of the archangel, and with the trump of God: and the dead in Christ shall rise first; then we that are alive, that are left, shall together with them be caught up in the clouds, to meet the Lord in the air: and so shall we ever be with the Lord." I remember a number of years ago in my study thinking about the coming of the Lord, contemplating what it will be to look on His lovely face, and the thought came to me: "I wonder what He will say to us all." And I began to thumb through my Bible to see if there was any suggestion that might be applicable to the question I was raising. Ultimately I turned to the book of the Song of Solomon, and I found what I believe may well be what the Lord will say to us all when He returns.

Now please, I understand that the Song of Solomon is a book all by itself, and I agree that it is the story of an actual courtship which has been preserved for us because of its spiritual application; and it tells us something of the love of the Lord and what our love for the Lord ought to be. And the narrative with all of its Orientalisms, vivid and startling to the Occidental, ought to be read with the realization that it presents not simply a courtship but another love which is higher, holier, and fuller than all. Let me also acknowledge that what I read and the application I will make of it is not its primary thrust. I know something of the movement of the book. But I want to take a section of chapter 2 and think about it as suggestive of what the Lord Jesus may say to you and me when He comes again. I recognize that the primary thrust has its relationship to the lover and the one loved in the book. I recognize also that there are applications of it which impinge upon our relationship to the Lord. But let me take it from its context, and let me apply it specifically to the Lord at His coming for His own.

In verse 8, chapter 2 of the book of Song of Solomon the bride is speaking. She says, "The voice of my beloved! behold, he cometh." Now if I need to prove anything, I think the application, even though it's secondary, that I am making, is fully substantiated by the words I have just read. "Behold, he cometh, leaping upon the mountains, skipping upon the hills. My beloved is like a roe or a young hart: Behold, he standeth behind our wall; he looketh in at the windows; he glanceth through the lattice. My beloved spake, and said unto me"—that's what I'm after. "My beloved spake, and said unto me," reports the bride, "Rise up, my love, my fair one, and come away. For, lo, the winter is past; the rain is over and gone; the flowers appear on the earth; the time of the singing of birds is come, and the voice of the turtle-dove is heard in our land; the fig tree ripeneth her green figs, and the vines are in blossom; they give forth their fragrance. Arise, my love, my fair one, and come away. O my dove, that art in the clefts of the rock, in the covert of the steep place, let me see thy countenance . . . thy countenance is comely."

There are just three things I would like to bring to your attention in connection with this message. First of all, it seems to me that the word the Lord speaks to the bride is an expression of an invitation. In the second place, it is the expression of the cessation of trial. And third, it is the expression of deepest love and holiest ardor.

It is the expression of an invitation. You notice it in verse 10: "Rise up, my love, my fair one, and come away." You see it again in verse 13, the end of the verse: "Arise, my love, my fair one, and come away." It seems to me this is very suitable language for our Lord as He comes. We are told in 1 Thessalonians 4:16 that He will shout. What will He shout? Well, perhaps it's this: "Rise up, my love, my fair one, and come away." He will speak to us. You'll remember that the Lord is the Lord Himself who descends from heaven, and He speaks: "Rise up, my fair one, my beloved, and come away."

I think we have a suggestion of this also in the book of Revelation in chapter 4 where we begin the section of the epistle which has to do with the coming days. John says, "After these things I saw, and behold, a door opened in heaven, and the first voice that I heard, a voice as of a trumpet speaking with me, one saying, Come up hither." And that experience of John has been taken by many of us as exemplary of what will happen when the Lord comes for us. He will say, "Come up hither," or in the language of the Song of Solomon, "Rise up, my love, my fair one, and come away." So it is the sound of His voice for which we wait.

And did you notice in the Song of Solomon two epithets are used, two appellations are used: "my love, my fair one." In thinking about that, I remembered how that on occasion the Lord would repeat a name, not just content to use one expression, but in repetition to speak a name twice. For example, in the twenty-second chapter of Genesis, the story of Abraham and Isaac. You'll recall that they were living in Beersheba, and God's word came to Abraham. And so he left Beersheba and made his way northward to the land of Moriah, and he took with him Isaac, his son, and his servants. He took with him the wood for a fire and made his way northward to the vicinity of Jerusalem, perhaps to the very place where the Temple later stood. And as he made his way there, you will recall Isaac plaintively asked the question: "I see the wood, I see the fire; but where is the lamb?" And you will recall how that when they got to Moriah, Abraham built an altar and laid the wood in order, and then was stayed in what he was about to do in giving Isaac as a sacrifice.

Let me read it for you: "And they came to the place which God had told him of; and Abraham built the altar there, and laid the wood in order, and bound Isaac his son, and laid him on the altar, upon the wood. And Abraham stretched forth his hand, and took the knife to slay his son. And the angel of Jehovah called unto him out of heaven, and said, Abraham, Abraham: and he said, Here am I. And he said, Lay not thy hand upon the lad, neither do thou anything unto him; for now I know that thou fearest God, seeing thou hast not withheld thy son, thine only son, from me." The angel of the Lord, a preincarnate manifestation of the second person of the holy Trinity, stayed the hand of

Abraham, but spoke his name: "Abraham, Abraham." I've often tried to think of how that name was spoken. I think there must have been infinite tenderness in it and very wonderful recognition of the faith of Abraham. God spoke his name twice. And so when He comes for His own He'll say: "My love, my fair one."

Or do you recall how that in the desert of Sinai, at Mount Horeb, there was a man by the name of Moses who in reverie was keeping the sheep of his father-in-law, Jethro. And as he sat there alone, suddenly he became aware of a phenomenon that was beyond his experience. He saw a bush that burned and was not consumed. And as he went to draw near, God spoke to him.

Let me read it for you. In the third chapter of the book of Exodus, there is this word: "God called unto him out of the midst of the bush, and said, Moses, Moses . . . Draw not nigh hither: put off thy shoes from off thy feet, for the place whereon thou standest is holy ground. . . . I am the God of . . . Abraham, the God of Isaac, and the God of Jacob. And Moses hid his face . . . and Jehovah said, I have surely seen the affliction of my people . . . and have heard their cry by reason of their taskmasters; for I know their sorrows; and I am come down to deliver them." But all of this was addressed to the man Moses, and the name was repeated: "Moses, Moses."

Or go with me much later to Shiloh and to the Tabernacle of God, to the days when Eli was the high priest. Remember there was a little lad who didn't know the Lord, who had been left at Shiloh to tend the needs of Eli and to be instructed and trained by the high priest. His name was Samuel, and God spoke to Samuel, and Samuel didn't know who it was that spoke to him. You remember the story, how he went to Eli, thinking it was Eli who spoke to him. And Eli finally, after Samuel had come to him three times, said to him, "It's the Lord, and this is the way you shall answer." You'll see it in chapter 3 of the book of 1 Samuel and verse 10. "And Jehovah came, and stood, and called as at other times, Samuel, Samuel. Then Samuel said, Speak; for thy servant heareth." It seems to be a custom of the Lord to repeat the name.

Sometimes He doesn't. I remember the scene in the garden at the time of the resurrection, when Mary stood alone; she went and looked into the tomb and saw two angels in white apparel, one at the head and one at the foot of the tomb, and the tomb was empty. And she turned around to leave the tomb, and she was aware that someone whom she thought was the gardener was standing there. And the angel said, "Why weepest thou?" And she gave the answer, thinking the Lord was the gardener; she said, "Where have you laid him?" Then the Lord said just one word: He said, "Mary." Oh, that I could have the intonation and the modulation of voice to express it the way He did. For immediately she knew who it was. And immediately she said, "Rabboni," my Teacher, my Master.

You remember how that on the shores of the Lake of Galilee the disciples had gathered, and the Lord was there. The Lord invited them to come from their fishing, and He said, "Simon, son of John, lovest thou me?"

So He's coming someday. I believe He'll call us by name. "My love, my fair one." I remember a verse I was taught by my mother that even as a lad brought great comfort to my heart, and through the years, again and again, God has used it to quiet my soul and to give rest to my spirit. Listen to it: "Fear not, I have redeemed thee, I have called thee by thy name, thou art mine." The Lord knows our names. We are of more value than many sparrows, and even the very hairs of our head are numbered. And so when he comes again, there's going to be the expression of an invitation: "Rise up, my love, my fair one, and come away."

There is a second thing here: the expression of the cessation of trial, beautifully expressed: "For, lo, the winter is past; the rain is over and gone; the flowers appear on the earth; the time of the singing of birds is come, and the voice of the turtle-dove is heard in our land." The winter is past; the rain is over and gone. Haven't you ever longed for the winter to be past? Haven't you ever, from the depths of your heart, cried out to God for the end of the rain? He's going to say, when He comes again, "The winter is past, the rain is over and gone."

Friends of mine are rather critical of David when, in the fifty-fifth Psalm, it is recorded that he said, "Oh, that I had wings like a dove, then would I fly away, and be at rest." Long since, I've given up any criticism of David for that. I've been there myself. Oh, that I had the wings of a dove! Bless your heart, someday He's coming, and the winter will be past; the rains will be over and gone. The winter with all its cold and blasted hopes, its long nights, will be ended; and the rains of adversity, the storms of

21

distress, the torrents of grief and tears will be over and gone. When He comes again, "the winter is past." He'll say, "The rains are over and gone."

> The sands of time are sinking,
> The dawn of Heaven breaks;
> The summer morn I've sighed for,
> The fair sweet morn awakes.
> Dark, dark hath been the midnight,
> But dayspring is at hand,
> And glory, glory dwelleth
> In Immanuel's land.

I'm speaking to some of you, and you're passing through the valley, and you're tempted to be despondent. May I remind you, the Lord is coming; and when the Lord comes, the winter is past, and the rain is over and gone. And then we'll be able to say, in the lovely words of Samuel Rutherford:

> With mercy and with judgment
> My web of time He wove,
> And aye the dews of sorrow
> Were lustered by His love;
> I'll bless the hand that guided,
> I'll bless the heart that planned,
> When throned where glory dwelleth,
> In Immanuel's land.

Oh, there's so much I don't understand now. There's so much I can't explain. I found out early in my ministry that I had no answers for many of the trials and testings that came to my people, except—God knows; God cares. And even if I can't prove it, it is so, that He makes all things work together for good. I remember the first time I turned to a dear soul deep in bereavement and said, "The verse says, 'we know,' not 'we understand'; we know that all things work together." And we know it not because we can dissect it, not because we can analyze it, not because we have smooth answers for all the questions unbelievers ask; no, we know it because we know Him, that's why. And He cannot be false to any of His children. The winter is past; the rain is over and gone.

But may I in faithfulness say to you, that's not all that will be over and gone. Thank God, we're looking for heaven and the presence of the Lord, but we have some privileges now that are going to be over when He comes. May I remind you that you will not increase in faith after you've seen Him, because faith will give place to sight. You'll no longer be able to sing,

'Tis so sweet to trust in Jesus,
Just to take Him at His word,
Just to rest upon His promise,
Just to know, "Thus saith the Lord."
Jesus, Jesus, how I trust Him,
How I've proved Him o'er and o'er!
Jesus, Jesus, precious Jesus,
Oh, for grace to trust Him more!

But you see, you're going to be home; and all that you have in faith will come to pass. Oh, how God speaks to me about this. I have the privilege even in the dark hours of earth's experience to put my hand in the hand of my Father and say, "Even so, Father, for it seemeth right in thine eyes." God wants, God longs to be trusted. He that cometh to God must believe, must believe that He is, and that He's a rewarder of them that diligently seek Him. But you'll not need to have faith, because it's all realized in the glory. That's the reason God speaks to my own heart again and again that when He allows trials to come and testing to come, and William Culbertson begins to groan and grieve and complain, I hear my Father say, "Son, this is your opportunity of opportunities to walk with Me and to know My presence the way you'll never know it in any other experience." Increase of faith will be over.

Growth in grace will be over, because when we see Him we shall be like Him. But oh, the thrilling exhilaration of walking day by day with the Lord and finding that He's leading me on in the knowledge of Himself and in fellowship with himself. Growth in grace ends in perfection, for then we shall know even as we are known.

Bless God, I have some privileges now, and even though my eyes are blinded with tears, and even though I have no explanation for what the Lord has allowed to come into my life in the way of suffering and trial, this I know: I can trust Him and He'll be pleased. It's easy to go along when things are well; but oh, when the dark clouds come, and when the night comes, just to walk with Him. I'd rather walk in the dark with God than walk alone in the light. I think you know what I'm talking about, those of you who know me. Increase in faith is over when He comes, because where you and I shall be by the grace of God, only saved people will be. The winter is past; the rain is over and gone. And all the heartaches and all the sorrow will be over.

One thing more. It is the expression of deepest love and holiest ardor. Think of Him, think of the Lord saying to you and to me: "my love, my fair one." Think of Him saying, "O my dove, that art in the clefts of the rock, in the covert of the steep place, let me see thy countenance, let me hear thy voice; for sweet is thy voice, and thy countenance is comely."

I was greatly blessed years ago in reading in *Daily Light* the selection for the day of April tenth. The family that brought together the texts for *Daily Light* brought together texts in contrast for that day. Listen to them; this is my confession: "Behold, I was shapen in iniquity, and in sin did my mother conceive me." But what does my lovely Lord say to me? That's my confession; that's true of William Culbertson naturally, but what does He say? This is what He says: "Thy renown went forth among the heathen for thy beauty, for it was perfect through my comeliness which I had put upon thee, saith the Lord God." My confession, His evaluation. Again, my confession: "I am a sinful man, O Lord." What does He see as He sees me? "Behold, thou art fair, my love; behold thou art fair." My confession: "I abhor myself, and repent in dust and ashes." But His word is: "Thou art all fair, my love, there is no spot in thee." Hallelujah! The blood of Jesus Christ, God's Son, keeps on cleansing us from all sin. So, thank God for this expression of deepest love. Listen: "Sweet is thy voice," He says; "comely is thy countenance." Oh, the wonder of it, the grace of it! Do you wonder why I love Him? I think I have a number of favorite hymns, but none is more meaningful to me than the worship and adoration expressed first of all by Bernard of Clairvaux in these words:

> Oh Jesus, King most wonderful,
> Thou Counsellor renowned,
> Thou sweetness most ineffable,
> From Whom all joys abound.

He's coming again, and He's going to say, "Sweet is thy voice, comely is thy countenance."

I trust that this isn't just theoretical with you. The blessed Lord is coming. And when He comes, there'll be the expression of an invitation, and the expression of the cessation of trial, and the expression of deepest love and holiest ardor. I must close with this word. I quote Samuel Rutherford again:

> The bride eyes not her garment,
> But her dear bridegroom's face;
> I will not gaze at glory,
> But on my King of grace;
> Not at the crown He giveth,
> But on His pierced hands;
> The Lamb is all the glory
> Of Immanuel's land.

Let us pray.

We love thee, Lord Jesus. Thou hast first loved us and given Thyself to us. How we long for the day when this same Jesus shall so come in like manner as the disciples saw Him go into heaven, when the Lord Himself shall descend from heaven with a shout. Make, we pray Thee, this doctrine blessed to us, meaningful to us. May we live in the light of it: our lovely Lord is coming again. We pray in the name of the Lord Jesus. Amen.

V. Raymond Edman
1900-1967

V. *Raymond Edman was pastor, missionary, educator, world traveler, and author of twenty devotional books. As president of Wheaton College, his chapel talks there will long be remembered by
students and faculty alike. An annual encouragement to students
was his "It's Always Too Soon to Quit."*

*Dr. Edman found time to serve on many boards of Christian
organizations, lending his advice, counsel, and encouragement. He
was also a man of prayer, for many years rising at 3 in the
morning to spend time before the Lord. He prayed for every student
on campus by name.*

*On September 22, 1967, Dr. Edman gave his final chapel talk
at Wheaton College. He spoke on "The Presence of the King." His
last words were, "Over the years I have learned the immense value
of that deep, inner silence as David, the king, sat in God's presence
to hear from Him." Having said these words, Dr. Edman was
ushered into the presence of the King, his Lord.*

*"If Good Men Will Not . . ." was an address given by Dr.
Edman at the 1964 Wheaton College Homecoming. It is a plea for
the righteous to become involved as leaders and influencers in
society.*

If Good Men Will Not . . .

If good men will not assume the responsibilities and bear the burdens in any given project, then unworthy, perhaps even wicked individuals will climb to places of leadership to their own advantage and to the detriment and disadvantage of good people and good causes.

This is a basic principle of life, whether we consider a local community or the entire country, a local church or the entire constituency of a Christian organization, the conduct and content of the grade and high schools or the strength and stability of Christian colleges and seminaries. If good and godly men stand aloof from moral and societal obligations in matters civic or spiritual, social or educational, their dereliction of duty creates a vacuum to be filled by the ambitious and unprincipled.

A responsible citizenry is indispensable for national strength and security. Responsible Christians are absolutely essential to the continuance of sound faith and effective service in the cause of Christ at home and abroad. Indifference and irresponsibility on their part are destructive of good government and the impact of the gospel upon one's fellows or upon the nation as a whole.

There is a definite relationship between vital and vibrant Christianity and the well-being of the nation politically, socially, economically, and culturally. One reads with deep searchings of heart the sound observations made by the Reverend Doctor Jedidiah Morse of Charlestown, Massachusetts, in his sermon of April 25, 1799, on the text: "If the foundations be destroyed, what can the righteous do?" (Psalm 11:3). At that time our new Republic was entering its second decade of national existence under the new Constitution of 1787, which had replaced the Articles of Confederation aptly described by the founding fathers as being merely "a rope of sand." The new Constitution, under which we still allegedly function, was based squarely on sound political and spiritual principles which had been learned in the long struggle between the Thirteen Colonies and the mother country.

Christianity Essential to Freedom

The preacher stated positively: "Our dangers are of two kinds, those which affect our religion, and those which affect our government. They are, however, so closely allied that they cannot, with propriety, be separated. The foundations which support the interests of Christianity are also necessary to support a free and equal government like our own. In all those countries where there is little or no religion, or a very gross and corrupt one, as in Mahometan and Pagan countries, there you will find, with scarcely a single exception, arbitrary and tyrannical governments, gross ignorance and wickedness, and deplorable wretchedness among the people. To the kindly influence of Christianity we owe that degree of civil freedom, and political and social happiness, which mankind now enjoys. (In proportion as the genuine effects of Christianity are diminished in any nation, either through unbelief, or the corruption of its doctrines, or the neglect of its institutions; in the same proportion will the people of that nation recede from the blessings of genuine freedom, and approximate the miseries of complete despotism.) I hold this to be a truth confirmed by experience. If so, it follows, that all efforts made to destroy the foundations of our holy religion ultimately tend to the subversion also of our political freedom and happiness. Whenever the pillars of Christianity shall be overthrown, our present republican forms of government, and all the blessings which flow from them, must fall with them."

The parable of Jotham in the book of Judges, chapter 9, is an excellent illustration of the indispensable relationship between godliness and good government, and its lessons should be faced earnestly and fearlessly by us in this latter third of the twentieth century. All Scripture is indeed given by inspiration of God and all of it is profitable for us, and this lesson, almost hidden away in an obscure portion of the Old Testament, is as up-to-date as tomorrow morning's newspaper.

The setting of the parable is given in the closing verses of chapter 8. After forty years of unselfish and effective leadership of the tribes of Israel, Gideon had died. There was no one at the moment to step into the place of leadership, spiritual or political. The Israelites "remembered not the Lord their God, who had delivered them out of the hands of all their enemies on every side; neither showed they kindness to the house of Jerubaal, namely, Gideon, according to all the goodness which he had shewed unto Israel" (8:34, 35).

Spiritual apostasy and absence of patriotism always go together. Where there is ingratitude on the part of any people to Almighty God and also to the heroes of yesterday who earned our freedoms at the price of blood, then there is likewise irresponsibility with intrinsic dangers of despotism and national degradation.

In times like those of the Judges it did not take long for the potential tyrant to show himself. With subtlety and stealth, with insinuation and innuendo, Abimelech concealed his ambition and lust for power. The program he proposed so quietly, even in an offhand manner, seemed to be very plausible. He enquired, "Whither is better for you, either that all the sons of Jerubbaal, which are threescore and ten persons, reign over you, or that one reign over you?" Ostensibly he was looking out for the welfare of the people. Of course he did not state the facts accurately. Honesty and uprightness do not serve the purposes of those greedy for place and power. Gideon had stated plainly, "I will not rule over you, neither shall my son rule over you: the Lord shall rule over you" (8:23).

Atheism an Enemy to Truth

It was convenient for Abimelech to forget that principle laid down by the heroic and godly leader of yesterday. When will mankind learn the lesson, so large in human affairs, that one can never trust the word of an atheist? Because he has no basic concept of truth or truthfulness, he declares whatever serves his purpose. The bigger the lie and more loudly repeated, the better as far as he and his cause are concerned.

Strange to say, nevertheless, the pages of history show plainly that apostasy and absence of patriotism make any people to be putty in the hands of the willful and the wicked. The hearts of

Abimelech's contemporaries inclined to follow him because they believed his pretentious and altogether unprincipled propaganda. They even supported him with their finances in his rise to power (9:4). What a strange commentary on human credulity, and yet many still follow that same pattern of action.

In our generation, Communist elements have played upon the sympathies and gullibility of the people so that they have insidiously planted themselves in places of influence in order to divert finances designated for human welfare to causes designed for our national destruction. Alger Hiss, for example, became the president of one of the largest philanthropic foundations. Other convinced Communists, dedicated to the destruction of America, have been supported by funds contributed originally by loyal Americans.

Then there was the infamous "sale" of wheat to bolster the sagging economy of the Soviets who state publicly and continually that their basic project is to bury America. Patriotic American farmers protested against the project and stevedores on the eastern seaboard refused to load the ships until they were cajoled and compelled by the State Department. The "sale" (on credit at the expense of the American taxpayers and not for cash as was true in the Canadian transaction) was pushed through a reluctant Congress compelled to remain in session until Christmas Eve of 1963.

Abimelech knew how to cajole his unsuspecting fellow citizens. Revelation of his true self came later when, with his ragamuffin revolutionists, paid by the funds contributed by the citizens of the land, Abimelech murdered all the sons of Gideon, except Jotham, the youngest, who managed to escape. There were blood purges by the brutal and ambitious in those days as well as in the twentieth century. Likewise it was true then as now that there was little or no public reaction against such violence. Perhaps the men of Shechem agreed wholeheartedly with the tyrant, or at any rate they were in no position to oppose him, with the result that "all the men of Shechem gathered together, and all the house of Millo, and went, and made Abimelech king . . ." (9:6).

The Biblical Parable

Then Jotham spoke out boldly and publicly in rebuke of all the people. In language typical of the Middle East he spoke in a parable (9:8-15).

The trees went forth on a time to anoint a king over
them; and they said unto the olive tree, Reign thou over
us. But the olive tree said unto them, Should I leave my
fatness, wherewith by me they honour God and man, and
go to be promoted over the trees?

And the trees said to the fig tree, Come thou, and reign
over us. But the fig tree said unto them, Should I forsake
my sweetness, and my good fruit, and go to be promoted
over the trees?

Then said the trees unto the vine, Come thou, and
reign over us. And the vine said unto them, Should I
leave my wine, which cheereth God and man, and go to
be promoted over the trees?

Then said all the trees unto the bramble, Come thou,
and reign over us. And the bramble said unto the trees, If
in truth ye anoint me king over you, then come and put
your trust in my shadow: and if not, let fire come out of
the bramble, and devour the cedars of Lebanon.

The olive tree, the fig tree, and the vine are representative of
the best elements in society. They are typical of men whose
"fruits" or "works" are a blessing to mankind, honest men of
stature in the community and pillars in the economy, men en-
dowed with ability, experienced, educated, and trained. However,
in the parable each one was unwilling to assume the responsibilities and burdens of leadership. They were materialists and not
idealists, self-centered and not sacrificial of spirit, cowardly and
not courageous. They were able to fulfill the proffered assignment
but were unwilling to sacrifice their own interests for the welfare
of all. In that sad day when Israel needed a true leader under God
there were men of piety and platitudes but not of patriotism.
They enjoyed the blessings of free government but would not risk
their personal interests to bear its burdens. There were good and
godly men, but they were sadly lacking in civic responsibilities
and in a sense of the times in which they lived. For the heroic
dead and the heritage of freedom they held no gratitude.

In the parable of the tares (Matthew 13:24-30) the Lord Jesus
made the incisive comment that "while men slept, his enemy
came and sowed tares among the wheat. . . ." It is only when good
men are indifferent and unconcerned that error and injustice can
prevail. In Jotham's parable he was saying, in substance, that it is
when men are self-centered with only self-interest at heart that
the tyrant arises.

Righteous Leadership Necessary

Absence of patriotism always goes hand in hand with spiritual apostasy. It is the responsibility of Christians to know the basic principles both of the gospel of God and of good government, and to believe and to practice both. We are to be exemplary in conduct, consistent and contagious Christians deeply and inextricably involved in the cause of Christ. We are to be concerned for our fellowmen so that we are likewise involved in efforts for good government whether on the local, state, or national level. It is the responsibility of Christians to perform the duties of citizenship. Every political right we have demands a corresponding duty. There is the duty to vote, to be available for public office, and to serve the community or the nation with honesty and integrity, in the fear of God.

Furthermore, it is the moral and spiritual obligation of Christians to foster the strengthening of spiritual life in the land. The pages of history, sacred or secular, give many illustrations of the truth that where there is spiritual revival and the rise of righteousness there is the blessing of Almighty God upon that land, as in the days of the good king Asa (2 Chronicles 14, 15), and Jehoshaphat (2 Chronicles 20), and Hezekiah (2 Chronicles 29—32). The Great Awakening of the 1740s raised the spiritual level of the American Colonies and strengthened them for the desperate ordeal of the Revolutionary War. The nationwide revivals of 1857-58 strengthened the soul of America for the long years of the War between the States.

Spiritual Revival Renews Patriotism

Spiritual revival is desperately indispensable for the renewal of patriotism in our land and of American leadership in the world. The gospel of the Lord Jesus Christ which brings freedom from the power and penalty of sin will also strengthen the pillars of American freedom. Indifference and irresponsibility will continue to undermine faith in God and the freedom of this land which has been the "land of the free and the home of the brave."

If good men and godly men are derelict in their duty, then the unworthy and the wicked will rise to power for the destruction of freedom. The bramble spoke great swelling words of boastfulness: "If in truth ye anoint me king over you, then come and put your trust in my shadow: and if not, let fire come out of the bramble, and devour the cedars of Lebanon." The thorn bush was so small that it had no shadow of its own, or at best one so insignificant that only scorpions or perhaps a desert rat could find comfort in its shadow. For the bramble's anointing to high office there would, of necessity, be the use of olive oil in the ceremony (such was the custom in Israel), and the fig tree and the vine would be stripped of their fruit for the feasting that accompanied the coronation. That is, the olive tree, the fig tree, and the vine would pay dearly for their unwillingness to make the sacrifice necessary for leadership. If good men will not pay the price of responsible leadership, they will pay plenty in the destruction of their own freedoms.

The late John Stuart Mill made this pertinent observation:

> A people may prefer a free government; but if from indolence, or carelessness, or cowardice, or want of public spirit, they are unequal to the exertions necessary for preserving it; if they will not fight for it when directly attacked; if they can be deluded by the artifices used to cheat them out of it; if by momentary discouragement or temporary panic, or a fit of enthusiasm for an individual, they can be induced to lay their liberties at the feet of even a great man, or trust him with powers which enable him to subvert their institutions—in those cases they are more or less unfit for liberty.

If good men will not . . . they will not have their freedom nor be able to pass that heritage to their children.

33

D. Martyn Lloyd-Jones
1899-1981

Dr. D. Martyn Lloyd-Jones was born in Wales. He trained as a physician and at the age of twenty-three became chief clinical assistant to Sir Thomas Horder, the King's Physician. When he was twenty-seven years of age, he appeared as a debater, political enthusiast, dairyman's assistant, doctor, and preacher in a struggling Calvinistic Methodist Church in Wales.

By 1933, the press reported that Lloyd-Jones's preaching drew thousands to hear his message of the gospel in all parts of the principality.

In 1938, Dr. Lloyd-Jones preached his first sermon at Westminster Chapel in London to an audience "not less than 2,000." He became the assistant to Dr. Campbell Morgan who retired from the pulpit in 1939, making way for Dr. Lloyd-Jones to continue at Westminster until his death more than forty years later.

"But God . . ." is a sermon he preached at Westminster Chapel on Remembrance Sunday and is published by Banner of Truth (Edinburgh) in God's Way of Reconciliation, which contains his sermons on Ephesians 2.

The Christian Message to the World

"But God . . ." Ephesians 2:4

We now come to look at two wonderful words— "But God." These words obviously suggest a connection with something that has gone before. The word "but" is a conjunction, and yet it suggests always a contrast; and here we have the connection and the contrast. Look at them in their context: "And you hath he quickened, who were dead in trespasses and sins; wherein in time past ye walked according to the course of this world, according to the prince of the power of the air, the spirit that now worketh in the children of disobedience: among whom also we all had our conversation in times past, in the lusts of our flesh, fulfilling the desires of the flesh and of the mind; and were by nature the children of wrath, even as others. But God . . ."

With these two words we come to the introduction to the Christian message, the peculiar, specific message which the Christian faith has to offer to us. These two words, in and of themselves, in a sense contain the whole of the gospel. The gospel tells of what God has done, God's intervention; it is something that comes entirely from outside us and displays to us that wondrous and amazing and astonishing work of God which the apostle goes on to describe and to define in the following verses.

We shall take these words now in a general manner only. I do so for several reasons. One is that the text itself compels one to do so, but there are also certain special reasons for doing so. A charge frequently brought against the Christian message, and especially the evangelical form of that message, is that it is remote from life, that it is irrelevant to the immediate circumstances in which men and women find themselves. In other words, there is an objection on the part of some to the expository method of preaching the gospel; it is that it never seems to come to grips with the realities of the situation in which men and women find themselves from day to day, and that it is irrelevant to the whole world situation in which we find ourselves. I desire to show, therefore, that that charge is entirely unfounded; and further, that the idea that the business of Christian preaching is just to make topical references to contemporary events is, indeed, in a sense, to depart from the Christian message altogether. I would go so far as to say that there is nothing which really does deal with the contemporary situation save the Scripture, when its doctrines are understood, believed, and applied.

That is what I propose to do now. I want to show the relevance of the gospel on a day such as Remembrance Sunday when instinctively almost, and certainly as the result of what is happening in the world in which we live, our minds are compelled to face, and to think of, the general situation in addition to our own particular situations. And, claiming as I do that the gospel deals with the whole of man and with the whole of his life in this world, it is important that we should see what it has to say about, and to do with, the position in which we find ourselves.

You notice that the thing I am emphasizing is the all-importance of method. The many who do not think in a Christian and Biblical manner believe that the business of the Christian church on a day such as this is to announce, for instance, a subject such as "The Geneva Conference—Possibilities," and then go on to say what we think the statesmen should do. That, it seems to me, is entirely false and contrary to the Biblical method.

The Biblical method, rather, is to display God's truth, and then to show the relevance of that to any given situation. You do not start with the situation; you end with the situation. The Bible invites us at the outset to stop looking on the horizontal level, as it were, to stop merely looking at the world and at men; it invites us at the very beginning to lift up our eyes and to look at God. In other words, the whole case presented in the Bible from beginning to end is that life and man and the world simply cannot be understood until we see everything in the light of the truth about God, and in that context. Therefore we must start with the truth of God and only then go on to the immediate situation.

Let us proceed to show how that is done, and how it is done

in the very passage which we are considering. We have considered in detail these first three verses in this chapter, and we have been doing so in order that we might see what we ourselves are like by nature and what the world is like by nature. You cannot begin to solve the problems of mankind until you know the truth about man. How futile it is to attempt to do so apart from that. You must start with the character, the nature, the being of man. Instead of starting with international conferences and talk about contemporary events, we need to go much further back and ask, Well, now, what sort of a creature is man? Obviously all our conclusions and all our proposals are going to be governed by the answer to that question. If man is really an essentially good creature who only needs a little more instruction and knowledge and information, obviously the treatment is going to be comparatively simple. But if what the Apostle Paul says here about man as he is by nature, and without Christ, is true, then, equally obviously, treatment along such lines is going to be entirely hopeless, and to attempt it is sheer waste of time.

We must start with this doctrine. *What is true of man in sin?* What characterizes man as he is in sin without the grace of God? . . . Man is dead spiritually; he is governed by the Devil, who operates through the mighty spiritual forces under his command, which in turn produce and control the mind and the outlook of the world. That is the position of man. And the result is that man, dominated by that evil power, lives a life of trespasses and sins; indeed he has been born in such a way, as the result of his descent from Adam, that his very nature is fallen. He starts with a polluted nature. And finally he is under the wrath of God. That is the apostle's statement in the first three verses.

What then is the relevance of all that to the present situation; what has it to say to us as we face the whole world situation at this present time? It is clear that a number of things can be very easily deduced from this teaching.

The first is that here we are given *the only real and adequate explanation of why there are such occurrences as wars.* Why do we have them? Why is man guilty of this final madness? Why is it that men kill one another and have even gloried in war? Why? What is the explanation of it all? There is only one answer; it is because man is as the apostle describes him. It is not only the teaching of the Apostle Paul. You remember how James puts it in the fourth chapter of his epistle: "Whence come wars among you?"—and answers the question: "even of the lusts that war in your members." That is the cause of war. It is man in his fallen condition.

Now the realization of this truth and fact is absolutely vital for us as a starting-point. This is true of nations, it is true of classes, it is true of individuals. There is surely nothing which is quite so illuminating and contradictory as the way in which people think along one line when they are thinking of nations and along a quite different line when they are thinking of individuals. There is little point in talking eloquently about the sanctity of international contracts while you are dealing with people who break their own marriage contracts and other personal contracts, for nations consist of individuals. The nation is not something abstract, and we are not entitled to expect conduct from a nation which we do not find in the individual. All these things have to be taken together.

This is a principle that operates throughout society from top to bottom, from the individual to the nation, to the continent, to the whole world itself. The explanation of the state of the world according to the Bible is that man is governed by these desires of the flesh and of the mind. He is not so much interested in whether a thing is right or not; he is interested in the fact that he wants it, that he likes it, that he must have it. Of course we stand back aghast when a nation behaves like that. When Hitler walks in and annexes Austria we are horrified. Yes, people are horrified who do the very same thing in their personal lives. They do it in the matter of other men's wives; they do it in the matter of another man's post or position in business. It is the same thing exactly. There then is the principle. It is this lust that governs mankind. "Walking according to the course of this world," says the apostle, "we all had our conversation in times past in the lusts of the flesh, fulfilling the desires of the flesh and of the mind." The first deduction, therefore, is that here and here alone do we have an adequate explanation and understanding of why things are as they are.

The second deduction follows quite logically. It is that *while man continues to be thus governed, the world will continue to be as it is.* This is surely obvious. If it is the state of man in sin that has been responsible for the history of the past, obviously while man remains unchanged, the history of the future is going to be unchanged. Here we confront and come into collision with the optimism of the natural man who is always so sure and confident that somehow or another we in our generation can put things right. He feels that whereas all other generations who have gone before us have failed, we are in a different position, in a superior position. We are educated and cultured; we know whereas they did not know; we have advanced so much, we must succeed; we are going to succeed. But if you believe this Biblical doctrine of man in sin, you must see at once that is a fatal fallacy. If our troubles are due to the lusts that are in mankind in sin, and which control men, while they remain there will be wars. We have specific teaching to that effect from our Lord Himself, who said, "There will be wars and rumors of wars." He said also, "As it was in the days of Noah, so shall it be also in the days of the Son of man"; "Likewise also as it was in the days of Lot"—in Sodom— "even thus shall it be" (Luke 17:26-30). That is our Lord's view of history.

If we grasp this teaching, we shall be delivered at once from all the false enthusiasm and the false hopes of men who really believe that by bringing in some new organization you can outlaw war and banish it forever. The answer of the Bible is that you cannot do so while man remains unregenerate. Is this depressing? My reply is that whether it is depressing or not is not our concern; we should be concerned to know the truth.

The modern man claims to be a realist. He has objected to Christianity because, according to him, it does not face the facts. It is not realistic, he says; it is always "pie in the sky," and you go into your chapels and you shut yourselves off and do not face the facts of life. Yet when we give him the facts he objects on the grounds that they are depressing. It is the political and philosophical optimists who are not realists; it is the people who have never faced the facts about man in sin who are shutting their eyes and turning their backs upon reality. The Bible faces it all; it has a realistic view of life in this world, and it alone has it.

Now let us look at *the specific, direct teaching of the gospel.* What has the Christian message to say about this state and this condition, the explanation of which we have just been considering? The answer is that it says, "But God . . ." That is its message. What does that mean? The most convenient way of analyzing this matter is to put it first of all negatively and then positively.

I regret that I have to start with a negative again. I must do so, because so many forget these negatives, and thus deliver messages which cannot possibly be regarded as Christian at all. And yet they will be delivered in the name of Christianity and of the Christian church. I am profoundly convinced that what is keeping large numbers of people from Christ and from salvation, and from the Christian church, is this terrible confusion of which the church herself has been, and is, so guilty. There are many outside the church today because in the First World War the Christian church so frequently became a kind of recruiting office. Men were offended—and in a sense they were right to be offended. There are certain things which should never be confused. Let us note some of them.

What is this Christian message? We start by saying that *it is not a great appeal for patriotism*. That is not the Christian message. The Christian message does not denounce patriotism or say that there is anything wrong in it. The man is to be pitied who does not love his country and his nation. There is nothing in the Scriptures against that. It is God who has divided up the nations and defined their bounds and their habitations. It is God's will that there should be nations.

But it is not God's will that there should be nationalism, an aggressive nationalism. There is nothing wrong in a man honoring his own country and delighting in it. But it is utterly un-Christian to say, "My country right or wrong." That is always wrong, that is fatally wrong; that is a complete denial of the teaching of Scripture. Take this great apostle who wrote this very Epistle to the Ephesians. Here is a man who was a Jew, and if ever a man was proud of the fact of his nationality it was the Apostle Paul—"A Hebrew of the Hebrews, of the tribe of Benjamin . . ." He was once a narrow nationalist who despised others. The Gentiles were dogs, outside the pale.

But the thing in which he glories in this epistle, you remember, is this: "in whom ye also trusted." The Gentiles have come in, have been made "fellow heirs" with the Jews; the middle wall of partition has been broken down. "There is no longer Jew nor Gentile, barbarian, Scythian, bond nor free, male nor female; all are one in Christ." That is the Christian position. "But God . . ."

Here is the way to break down that nationalistic spirit that leads to war. To believe that we are always right and everybody else wrong is as wrong in nations as it is in individuals. It is always wrong. The Christian message is not just an appeal to patriotism. And if Christianity is portrayed in that form it is a denial, a travesty of the message, and it is misleading in the eyes and the ears of those who listen to it.

But secondly, *the Christian message is not just an appeal to courage or heroism* or to the manifestation of a great spirit of self-sacrifice. Let us be clear about this also. Christianity does not condemn courage; it does not condemn self-sacrifice or heroism. These qualities, these virtues are not specifically Christian. They are pagan virtues, which were taught and inculcated, admired and praised, before the Lord Jesus Christ ever came into this world. Courage was the supreme virtue according to the Greek pagan philosophers; it was the very essence of Stoicism. And that was why they regarded meekness, the meekness taught by the Christian faith, as weakness. There was no word for meekness in Greek pagan philosophy. Courage, and strength, and power—those were the things they believed in.

That is why, you remember, Paul tells us that the preaching of the cross was "to the Greeks foolishness." That someone who was crucified in weakness should be the Savior, and that that should be the way of salvation, to them was nonsense and rubbish. They placed no value on meekness and on humility; courage and power and heroism were the great virtues.

So it is very important that we should realize that it is no part of the Christian message to exhort people to courage and heroism and to self-sacrifice. There is nothing specifically Christian in such ideas. Christianity does not condemn them, but that is not the Christian message. And the point I am emphasizing is this, that when that has been presented as the Christian message it has confused people, and has led to the very division which the gospel itself was meant to heal.

But let us go on to a third matter. There are many people who seem to think that the Christian message is that we should just appeal to the world to put into practice the Christian principles. *Now this is the pacifist position, so-called.* They say, Now, you Christian people, you are always preaching about personal salvation and about doctrines and so on; why do you not do something about wars? Well then, we say, what do you want us to do? They reply, What you have to do is to tell the people to practice the Sermon on the Mount. Why do you not tell them to turn the other cheek and to love one another and so on, then there would be an end of war? You have the solution; just get people to put into operation the principles of the teaching of Christ.

What is the answer to that? The answer is the teaching of the first three verses in this second chapter of Paul's Epistle to the Ephesians. You can preach the Sermon on the Mount to people who are "dead in trespasses and sins" until you have exhausted yourself and you will be none the wiser; neither will they. They cannot practice it. They do not want to. They are "enemies and aliens in their minds." They are governed by "lusts." They "fulfill the desires of the flesh and of the mind." They are governed and ruled by this. How can they practice the Sermon on the Mount?

There is only one hope for man in sin, says Paul— "But God . . ." Men need to be regenerated; they must be given a new nature before they can even understand the Sermon on the Mount, leave alone begin to put into practice. So it is but a travesty of the Christian message to speak of it as if it were but an appeal to men to rise up and to follow Christ in their own strength and to put into operation Christian principles of teaching. It is as much a travesty of the gospel as is the preaching of patriotism and imperialism. It is equally non-Christian.

It is indeed dangerous heresy, the ancient Pelagian heresy, because it fails to realize that man, being what he is in sin, cannot possibly implement such teaching. To expect Christian conduct from people who are not yet Christians is dangerous heresy.

You see how important our teaching is, and how essential it is that we should be clear about the true application of the Christian message to the modern world. That is why we do not spend our time in talking about international conferences and about politics and international relationships or industrial disputes or in preaching always on the question of pacifism and against physical warfare. To do so is simply to waste time—though it would probably attract publicity. What is needed is that we should start with this fundamental principle, the doctrine of man in sin, in his deadness, in his hopelessness, in his complete helplessness.

To sum up at this point, the negative principle is that the Christian faith, the Christian gospel, has no direct message for the world except to say that the world as it is, is under the wrath of God, that it is under condemnation, and that all who die in that state will go to perdition. The only message of the Christian faith to an unbelieving world, in the first instance, is simply about judgment, a call to repentance, and an assurance that if they do repent and turn to Christ they shall be delivered. The church, therefore, the Christian faith, has no message to the world apart from that.

But the Bible also teaches very plainly and clearly that while that is the message of God to the unbelieving world, God nevertheless has done something about that unbelieving world. What He has done in the first instance is this. *He has put a control upon the power of sin and evil.* He has done so in this way.

As I have already reminded you, he has divided up the peoples of the world into nations. Not only so, He has ordained that there should be states and governments. He has ordained "the powers that be." "The powers that be," says Paul in Romans 13, "are ordained of God"; whether it be a king or an emperor or a president of a republic, "the powers that be are ordained of God."

It is God who has ordained magistrates and given them the sword of power. Why? Simply to keep the manifestations of evil within bounds and under control. For if God had not done this, if the lusts that operate in us all by nature and by inheritance from Adam were allowed unlimited and uncontrolled manifestation, the world would be hell, and it would have hurtled itself to perdition long ago and would have destroyed itself. God has put a limit upon it. He has put a bound even upon evil, He has held it in, He has restricted it.

Indeed, the Apostle Paul in a most extraordinary statement in the Epistle to the Romans (chapter 1, verses 18ff.) proves the matter by saying that sometimes, for His own end and purposes, God withdraws that restraint partially. He says that God "had given them over to a reprobate mind." There are times and seasons when God seems to relax the restraint that He has put upon sin and evil in order that we may see it in all its horror. It may well be that we are living at such a time. But that is what the Bible tells us about what God does directly about man in sin; He controls the manifestations of his foul and evil and fallen nature. That is the *general* message.

But what is the *particular* message? This is the thing that the apostle is concerned to emphasize most of all in this immediate paragraph. *The message to individuals is that we can be delivered out of this present evil world,* that we can escape the condemnation that is coming for certain upon this world. That is the message the apostle preached. It is a message to individuals. It does not say that the world can be put right if we only implement Christian teaching; it is not an appeal to people to reform themselves and to do this or that. No, it is a message which says that as the result of what God has done in Christ Jesus, His Son, our Lord and Savior, we who were in the very warp and woof of that sinful, condemned world can be delivered out of it. "Who gave Himself for our sins," he says to the Galatians, "that He might deliver us from this present evil world." The world is doomed, the world is going to be destroyed and punished, the Devil and all his forces are going to perdition, and all who belong to that realm will suffer the same punishment. But the message of the gospel to men and women individually is that they need not be participators in that. You can be taken out of it—"out of the kingdom of darkness," brought out from the power of Satan, unto God. That is its message to individual men and women. The world will remain as it is, but you can be delivered out of it, you can be taken out of it.

Not only that; we can also be introduced into and become citizens of a kingdom which is not of this world. As we go through this chapter we shall find Paul elaborating his own words. The marvelous thing, he says, is that you Gentiles are in Christ, and because of His blood, have become fellow-citizens with the saints; you have become citizens in the kingdom of God, the kingdom of Christ, the kingdom of light, the kingdom of heaven—a kingdom that is not of this world, a kingdom which cannot be shaken, a kingdom which cannot be moved. That is the kingdom into which we enter.

This is the most thrilling news a man can ever hear. Now we are all citizens of this country, our native land, and we are all involved in what happens to this country. If this country goes to war we shall be involved. We did not escape the bombs in the last war any more than anybody else simply because we were Christians. We are all involved in it; we are citizens of this world, and we share in the fate of this world. But thank God, here is something different. While remaining citizens of this world we become citizens of another kingdom, this other kingdom that has been opened to us by Christ—a spiritual kingdom, a kingdom that is not of this world, eternal in the heavens with God. That is the teaching of this message. "But God . . ."

The doctrine works itself out in practice like this. If I believe this message, from now on *I am not going to pin my hopes, nor rest my affections finally, on anything in this world.* The natural man does so, of course; he pins his hopes on this world and its mind, its outlook, its statesmen, its mentality, its pleasures, its joys. He lives for it, and all his hopes are centered here, his affections are here. Not so the Christian.

The Christian, having been given to see that this world is doomed, that it is under the wrath of God, has fled from "the wrath to come." He has believed the gospel, he has entered this other kingdom, and his hopes and affections are set there now, not here. The Christian is a man who, to use a Scriptural phrase, knows that he is but "a stranger and a pilgrim" in this world. He is a mere sojourner. He does not any longer live for this world: he has seen through it, he sees beyond it. He is but a journeyman, a traveler, and, as James puts it (chapter 4), he is a man who has realized that his life is "but a vapor," a breath. So he does not regard this world as permanent; he does not lay down his plans and say, I am going to do this or that. Not at all! But rather, "If the Lord will . . ."; it is all under God, and he realizes how contingent it is. He does not any longer pin his faith or set his affections on this world.

But still more marvelous! *He is never taken by surprise over anything that happens in this world.* That is why I said earlier that there is nothing that I know of that is so relevant to worldly circumstances as this gospel. The Christian is a man who is never surprised by what happens in the world. He is prepared for everything, prepared for anything. He is not at all surprised when a war breaks out.

The non-Christian, and especially the idealist, of course, is greatly surprised. He really did believe at the end of the First World War that the League of Nations was going to abolish war forever. There were many who believed that the Locarno Pact of 1925 was finally going to do it, and they were very happy. They were confident that there would never be another war like that of 1914-18. And when it came in 1939 they did not know how to explain it.

But the true Christian, knowing that man is a creature who is governed by lusts, and that lust always produces war, knew perfectly well no Locarno Pact or anything else could outlaw or abolish war. He knew that war might come at any time, and when it came he was not surprised. As Psalm 112 puts it in the seventh verse: "He shall not be afraid of evil tidings; his heart is fixed, trusting in the Lord."

45

Believing as we do this Biblical doctrine of man in sin, we should never be surprised at what happens in the world. Are you surprised at all the murders, the thefts, the violence, the robbery, all the lying and the hatred, all the carnality, the sexuality? Does it surprise you as you look at your newspapers? It should not do so if you are a Christian. You should expect it. Man in sin of necessity behaves like that. He cannot help himself; he lives, he walks in trespasses and sins. He does it individually, he does it in groups; therefore there will be industrial strifes and misunderstandings and there will be wars.

Oh, what pessimism! says someone. I say, No, what realism! Face it, be prepared for it, do not expect anything better from a world like this; it is a fallen, sinful, godless, evil world; and while man remains in sin, it will be like that. And it is as much like that today as it was in the days of Sodom and Gomorrah and in the time of the flood!

But, thank God, I have not finished. I go on to say that the Christian is a man who, realizing that he is living in such a world, and who, having no illusions at all about it, yet knows that he is linked to a Power that enables him not only to bear whatever may come to him in such a world, but indeed to be "more than conqueror" over it. He does not just passively bear it, he does not merely put up with it, he does not just "stick it" and exercise courage. No, that is stoicism, that is paganism. The Christian, being in Christ, the Christian knowing something of what the apostle calls "the exceeding greatness of God's power to us-ward that believe," is strengthened, is enabled to endure. His heart does not quail, he is not defeated; indeed, he can rejoice in tribulations. Let the world do its worst to him, let hell be let loose, he is sustained. "This is the victory that overcometh the world, even our faith." So that if things really do become impossible, the Christian has resources, he still has comforts and consolations, he still has a strength of which all others are ignorant.

Finally, the Christian is absolutely certain and assured that whatever the world and men may do *he is safe in the hands of God*. "We can confidently say," say the Scriptures, "the Lord is my helper, and I will not fear what man shall do unto me." Indeed he knows this, that man in his malignity may insult him, may persecute him, may ravage him, may even destroy his body; but he also knows that nothing shall ever be able to "separate [him] from the love of God which is in Christ Jesus our Lord." He knows that whatever may happen in this world of time, he is a son of God, an heir of glory. Indeed he knows this, that a day is coming when even this present sinful world shall be entirely redeemed, and there "shall be new heavens and a new earth wherein dwelleth righteousness."

The Christian can look forward to this, that he, some glorious day in the future, when his very body shall be renewed and glorified, when it shall no longer be weak, when it shall be no longer subject to sickness and old age and disease, when it will be a glorified body like that of the risen Christ—he knows that he in this glorified body shall even walk the face of this very earth, out of which evil and sin and vileness shall have been burned by the fire of God. He will dwell in a perfect world, of which the Lamb, the Son of God, is the Light and the Sun, the Brightness and the Glory, and he shall enjoy it forever and ever. That is what the Christian message, the Christian faith has to say to this wretched, distracted, unhappy, confused, frustrated, modern world. It is all the outcome of these essential doctrines which can be learned only in this Book which is God's Word. There is the world—"But God . . ."

Henry Allan Ironside
1878-1951

Henry Allan (Harry) Ironside read through the Bible at least once a year from the time he was eight years old. He began preaching immediately after his conversion at age fourteen and became known as the "boy preacher of Los Angeles."

After six years with the Salvation Army, he joined the Plymouth Brethren, preaching and doing Bible conference work throughout the United States, Canada, and the British Isles. He held meetings under the direction of Moody Bible Institute, was visiting professor at Dallas Theological Seminary, and was for eighteen years pastor at the Moody Memorial Church in Chicago. He authored more than sixty books, many of which were pulpit messages, lectures, and expositions of the books of the Bible.

"The Eternal Security of the Believer" was preached on a Friday night at the Moody Memorial Church. The next two Friday evenings were devoted to answering questions having to do with this message.

The Eternal
Security of
the Believer

Can a believer ever be lost?

It has been announced that I will speak to you on a subject which has occasioned a good deal of controversy among the people of God. I want to take as a starting-point—not exactly as a text, because we shall be looking at a good many Scriptures—Romans 8:38, 39: "For I am persuaded that neither death, nor life, nor angels, nor principalities, nor powers, nor things present, nor things to come, nor height, nor depth, nor any other creature, shall be able to separate us from the love of God, which is in Christ Jesus our Lord." This is the inspired answer to the question of verse 35: "Who shall separate us from the love of Christ?" That is, once we are Christians, once we know the love of Christ, once we have been justified by faith, who is there, what power is there, that can separate from the love of Christ? And the answer, how full, how clear, not a shadow, not a doubt, not a question left, when the apostle says that neither death nor life shall separate! Can you think of anything which is neither included in death nor in life? Neither death nor life shall separate!

Then, no unseen powers can separate the believer from Christ—"Neither angels, nor principalities, nor powers." These terms are used again and again in the New Testament, particularly in the epistles, for angelic hosts, good and evil. When our Savior rose from the dead, He spoiled principalities and powers; that is, He defeated all the hosts of evil led by Satan. And so we may take it that the angels referred to here are good angels, and the principalities and powers are possibly evil angels. But there is nothing that good angels would do, and nothing that evil angels can do, which will result in the separation of the believer from Christ.

And then further, he says, "Neither things present nor things

49

to come." Again let me put the question, Can you think of any experience through which a believer might ever go which is neither a thing present nor a thing to come? And the Holy Ghost says that neither things present nor things to come shall be able to separate us from the love of Christ. As though that were not enough, He speaks in a more general way when he says that neither "height nor depth (nothing in heaven, nothing in hell), nor any other created thing, shall be able to separate us from the love of God, which is in Christ Jesus our Lord." It looks to me as though we are pretty safe if we are believers in the Lord Jesus Christ.

Eternal Security: Its Meaning

When we speak of the eternal security of the believer, what do we mean? We mean that once a poor sinner has been regenerated by the Word and the Spirit of God, once he has received a new life and a new nature, has been made partaker of the divine nature, once he has been justified from every charge before the throne of God, it is absolutely impossible that that man should ever again be a lost soul.

Having said that, let me say what we do *not* mean when we speak of the eternal security of the believer. We do not mean that it necessarily follows that if one professes to be saved, if he comes out to the front in a meeting, shakes the preacher's hand, and says he accepts the Lord Jesus Christ as his Savior, that that person is eternally safe. It does not mean that if one joins a church or makes a profession of faith, is baptized, becomes a communicant, takes an interest in Christian work, that that person is forever secure. It does not mean that because one manifests certain gifts and exercises these gifts in Christian testimony, that that person is necessarily eternally secure.

Our Lord Jesus Christ said to the people of His day, as recorded in Matthew 7:21-23, "Not every one that saith unto Me, Lord, Lord, shall enter into the kingdom of heaven; but he that doeth the will of My Father which is in heaven. Many will say to Me in that day, Lord, Lord, have we not prophesied in Thy name? and in Thy name have cast out devils? and in Thy name done many wonderful works? And then will I profess unto them, I never knew you: depart from Me, ye that work iniquity." Such people then may have been very active in what is called Christian work—they have preached, they have cast out demons (that is, their influence has been such that men and women have found deliverance from Satanic power through their ministrations in the name of Jesus), they have professed with their lips, they have accomplished many wonderful works. But they are found in that day among the lost, and when they plead their great activity and their earnestness in Christian testimony, the Lord says to them, "I never knew you." Notice, He does not say to them, "I used to know you, but you have forfeited My favor and I do not know you any longer." He says, "I *never* knew you."

The Sheep of Christ

You remember how He speaks of His own in John 10:27-30: "My sheep hear My voice, and I know them, and they follow Me: and I give unto them eternal life; and they shall never perish, neither shall any man pluck them out of My hand. My Father, which gave them Me, is greater than all; and no man is able to pluck them out of My Father's hand. I and My Father are one." Of His own He says, "I know them."

Of these others, in spite of all their activity, in spite of all their accomplishments, He says in the day of judgment, "I never knew you." That is a very solemn thing. That answers a question that is frequently put to us. I do not know how many times I have had individuals come to me with a hypothetical case like this: "Suppose a man who joined the church, who professed to be saved, who for a number of years was a very active Christian worker, perhaps a Sunday school teacher, perhaps an elder or a deacon in the church, maybe a minister, but after some years of apparent consistent Christian living and helpfulness in testimony he turns his back on it all, returns to the world, and utterly repudiates Christianity and now denies in toto the gospel he once professed. How does that square with your doctrine of the eternal security of the believer?" That does not touch the matter at all.

The Apostle John tells us how we are to understand a case like that. He says in the second chapter and the nineteenth verse of his first epistle, "They went out from us, but they were not of us; for if they had been of us, they would no doubt have continued with us: but they went out, that they might be made manifest that they were not all of us," or literally, "that they were not altogether of us." That is, it is possible to do all the things that I have spoken of and yet never be regenerated. It is quite possible to join a church, to make a Christian profession; it is quite possible to observe the Christian ordinances, to teach and preach, and yet never be born again. If one teaches and preaches the truth, it will produce good results, and will do men good whether the teacher or the preacher be real or not, for it is the truth that God uses.

Of course He can use the truth to better advantage when it is proclaimed by a holy man living to the glory of God than when it is proclaimed by a hypocrite. Nevertheless, God uses His truth regardless of who may proclaim it, and that explains how people may do mighty works in the name of Christ and yet never be born again.

Christ's One Offering

When we say that the believer in the Lord Jesus is eternally secure, we base it upon a number of lines of Scriptural testimony. In the first place, we rest upon the perfection of Christ's one offering upon the cross. Personally, I never can understand how thoughtful people, taught by the Holy Spirit of God, can carefully read the Epistle to the Hebrews and not see that throughout that epistle the writer is contrasting the many sacrifices offered under law with the one sacrifice of our Lord Jesus Christ.

That to which he particularly calls attention is this: under law every time an Israelite sinned, he needed a new sin offering, and every year the nation had to celebrate the great day of atonement when a new offering was presented to God for the people. Why? Because those sacrifices could never take away sin; they simply covered sin for the time being.

But we are told in the tenth chapter of Hebrews that when the Lord Jesus Christ came unto the world and offered Himself without spot to God, the effect of His sacrifice was eternal. Verse 14 makes this clear: "For by one offering He hath perfected for ever them that are sanctified." Perfected for how long? "Oh," says somebody, "as long as they are faithful." No, that is not what it says. "He hath perfected for ever." Why? Because the sacrifice is all-efficacious.

I am sure my brethren who deny the doctrine of the eternal security of the believer do not realize that in so doing, they are putting a slight upon the finished work of Christ, they are reducing the sacrifice of Christ practically to the level of the offerings of bulls and goats in the Old Testament dispensation. I am sure they do not mean to do that, for they love their Lord just as truly as I trust I love Him, and they do not want to dishonor Him. But they are afraid that this doctrine will lead people to be careless about their lives, and therefore they stress the possibility of a man losing his salvation after he has once been justified by faith. But they do not pursue that to the logical conclusion, they do not see that it is a practical denial of the finished work of our Lord Jesus Christ. We are saved eternally because the sacrifice of Christ abides.

When I came to the Lord Jesus Christ and put my trust in Him, not only were all my sins up to the day of my conversion forgiven, but all my sins were put away for eternity. When a young Christian, I was taught something like this: I thought when I was converted that all my sins, from the time of dawning accountability up to that night when I put my trust in the Lord Jesus, were put away, and now God had given me a new start, and if I could only keep the record clean to the end of my life, I would get to heaven; but if I did not keep it clean, I ceased to be a Christian and I had to get converted all over again. Every time this happened the past was under the blood, but I had to keep the record clean for the future.

What a God-dishonoring view of the atonement of Christ that is! If only those of my sins that were committed up to the moment of my conversion were put away by the atoning blood of Jesus, what possible way would there be by which sins I have confessed after that could be dealt with? The only ground on which God could forgive sin is that Jesus settled for all upon the cross, and when I trust Him, all that He has done goes down to my account.

What of Future Sins?

A lady came to me one day and said, "I do not get you there. I can quite understand that Christ died for the sins I committed up to the night of my conversion, but do you mean to tell me that Christ died for my future sins?"

I said, "How many of your sins were in the past when Christ died on the cross?"

She looked puzzled for a moment, and then the light broke

in, and she said, "How foolish I have been! Of course they were all future when Christ died for me. I had not committed any of them."

God saw all your sins, and He laid upon Jesus all your iniquity, and therefore when you trusted Him, you were justified freely from all things. Do you say, "Does it make no difference then if a believer sins?" That is another question, and it would take a whole evening to go into that, but here is the point—the moment you trust the Lord Jesus as your Savior, your responsibility as a sinner having to do with a Father in heaven begins. Now if as a child you should sin against your Father, God will have to deal with you about that, but as a Father and not as a Judge. That is a line of truth that stands by itself and does not contradict what I am now teaching. It explains some things that bewilder people when this doctrine is brought before them.

The Spirit's Perseverance

In the second place, we base the doctrine of the eternal security of the believer upon the perseverance and omnipotent power of the Holy Spirit of God. Look at the first chapter of the Epistle to the Philippians. Writing to these saints, the apostle says, when he thanks them for their fellowship in the gospel from the first day until now, "Being confident of this very thing, that he which hath begun a good work in you will perform it until the day of Jesus Christ." Do you see that? Who began the good work in you if you are a believer in the Lord Jesus? The Holy Spirit of God. It was He who convicted you of sin, it was He who led you to put your trust in Christ, it was He who through the Word gave you the witness that you were saved, it is He who has been conforming you to Christ since you first trusted the Lord Jesus.

Having thus taken you up in grace, the Holy Spirit has a definite purpose in view. He is going to eventually conform you fully to the image of the Lord Jesus Christ, and He never begins a work that He does not intend to finish. "Being confident of this very thing, that he which hath begun a good work in you will perform it until the day of Jesus Christ." If when you were a poor sinner the Holy Spirit had power sufficient to break down your opposition to God and to bring to an end your unbelief and rebellion, do you think for one moment that He does not have power enough to subdue your will as a believer and to carry on to completion the work that He began?

People say, "I see you believe in that old Baptist doctrine of 'once in grace, always in grace.' " Or another says, "I understand you hold that old Presbyterian idea of 'the final perseverance of the saints.' " I do not know why this should be called either Baptist or Presbyterian, only to the extent that Baptists and Presbyterians agree with the Book. The Word of God clearly shows that once God takes us up in grace, nothing can separate us from the love of Christ; so that evidently the expression, "Once in grace, always in grace" is a perfectly correct one.

But, on the other hand, I am not so enthusiastic about the other expression, "the perseverance of the saints." I believe in it; I believe that all saints, all really belonging to God, will persevere to the end, for the Book tells me, "He that shall endure unto the end, the same shall be saved" (Matthew 24:13). If a man starts out and makes a profession but gives it all up, he will never be saved, because he was never born again to begin with, he was never truly changed by grace divine. On the other hand, the reason he endures to the end is not because of any particular perseverance of his own. What I believe in, and what the Word of God clearly teaches, is the perseverance of the Holy Spirit. When He begins a work, He never gives up until it is completed. That is our confidence.

Experience and Faith

Forty-three years ago the Spirit of God in grace led me to trust the Lord Jesus Christ. I have had many ups-and-downs since then, as the old folks used to sing in a camp meeting I attended:

I am sometimes up and sometimes down,
But still my soul am heavenly bound.

I have had varied experiences, but the wonderful thing is this: the Holy Spirit of God has never given me up; and if at times I have been wayward and willful and did not immediately bow before God and repent of my waywardness and willfulness, then I found I had come under the rod, my Father's rod, and He whipped me into subjection until I came to the place where I was ready to confess my failure and be restored to fellowship with Him. But I was just as truly His child while getting a good whipping as I was when the effects of it had restored me to fellowship. Your child does not cease to be your child when you have him over your knee and are using the slipper on him. It is because he is your child, and because you want him to grow up to be a well-behaved boy, that you do that.

And so we believe in the perseverance of the Holy Spirit of God, that having begun the work He will carry it on to completion.

New Creation

In the third place, we base the doctrine of the eternal security of the believer upon the fact of the new creation. In the fifth chapter of Second Corinthians, verse seventeen, we read: "Therefore if any man be in Christ, he is a new creature: old things are passed away, behold, all things are become new." That verse may be rendered like this: "Therefore if any man be in Christ, this is a new creation; old things have passed away, and all things have become new."

What do we mean by *new creation?* Just this: we were once in the place of death, we were once utterly lost and ruined. How did we get there? Follow me now. It was not by any act of our own. Do you say, "I did not get into the place of spiritual death by any act of my own"? No, you did not. Do you say, "I was not lost because of any act of my own"? No, you were not. But why were you numbered among the lost? Because you were born into the world a member of the old creation of which Adam the first was the head, and every child of Adam's race comes into the world lost and is under sentence of death. And so we read in this same chapter in verse 14, "The love of Christ constraineth us; because we thus judge, that if One died for all, then were all dead."

The Two Adams

Let me try to make that clear. Here is Adam the first, the head of the old creation, and he was placed on trial in the Garden of Eden. The entire world was represented in him—you were represented in him, I was represented in him. As the Spirit of God says of Levi, "He was yet in the loins of his father, when Melchisedec met him" (Hebrews 7:10), so we, every one of us, were represented there in Adam when the old creation was on trial. Adam failed, and God said, "In the day thou eatest thereof, dying thou shalt die." As a result of that failure the old creation fell down in death, and every person that has ever been born in the world since that time was born down there; no one has been born up here, where Adam the first started, except our Lord Jesus Christ, and His birth was a supernatural one.

Therefore, as members of the old creation we were all dead, all lost; but now see what happened. Our Lord Jesus Christ came into the world—the written Word here speaks of Him as the living Word—and He stood on this plane of sinlessness. Adam was created sinless but fell; Jesus came, the sinless One, conceived of the Holy Ghost, born of a virgin mother, but He saw men down there in death, and at the cross He went down into death, down to where man was, and came up in grace from death. But He did not come up alone, for God quickened us together with Christ, so that all who believe in Him are brought up from that place of death; and as at one time we were made partakers of Adam's race, so now we are made partakers of a new creation.

What does God do for us now? Does He put us where Adam was before and say, "Now behave yourselves, and you won't die again"? No, He puts us up higher than Adam could ever have gone except by a new and divine creation. "He hath raised us up together, and made us sit together in heavenly places in Christ Jesus" (Ephesians 2:6), and because we belong to this new creation we can never be lost. You were lost because the head of the old creation failed, and you went down with him. You can never be lost unless the Head of the new creation falls, and if He does you will go down with Him. But, thank God, He remains on the throne where God Himself has put Him, in token of His perfect satisfaction in the work He accomplished.

You may have heard of the Irishman who was converted but was seized with a dreadful fear that someday he might commit some great sin and lose his soul, that he might be lost after all, and he trembled at the thought. He went to a meeting and heard the words read, "Ye are dead, and your life is hid with Christ in God." "Glory to God!" shouted Pat; "whoever heard of a man drowning with his head that high above water?" We are linked with Him, we belong to the new creation, and that is why we shall never be lost.

Eternal Life Possessed Now

In the last place, we rest the truth of the doctrine of the eternal security of the believer upon the fact that the believer is the present possessor of eternal life. It is not merely that if we are faithful to the end we *shall* receive eternal life. There is a sense in which that is true; there is a sense in which our hope is eternal life. I am a Christian now if I believe on the Lord Jesus Christ; believing on Him I have eternal life, but I have it in a dying body. I am now waiting for the redemption of the body, and when the Lord Jesus comes the second time He shall change this body of my humiliation and make it like unto the body of His glory. Then I shall have received eternal life in all its fullness, spirit, soul, and body entirely conformed to Christ. In that sense I am hoping for eternal life.

But over and over and over again, Scripture rings the changes on the fact that every believer is at the present time in possession of eternal life. "As Moses lifted up the serprent in the wilderness, even so must the Son of Man be lifted up; that whosoever believeth in him should not perish, but *have* eternal life" (John 3:14, 15). Adam's life was forfeitable life; he lost his life because of sin. Eternal life is nonforfeitable life; otherwise it would not be eternal. "For God so loved the world, that he gave his only begotten Son, that whosoever believeth in him should not perish, but have everlasting life" (John 3:16).

Everlasting life is life that lasts forever, and we have it now. "He that believeth on the Son hath everlasting life: and he that believeth not the Son shall not see life; but the wrath of God abideth on him" (John 3:36). "Verily, verily, I say unto you, He that heareth My word, and believeth on him that sent me, hath everlasting life, and shall not come into condemnation; but is passed from death unto life" (John 5:24).

His Sheep Shall Follow Him

I have purposely left this point until last because people generally take it for granted it will be the first passage used in taking up this subject. In John 10, reading from verse 27, we are told, "My sheep hear my voice, and I know them, and they follow me."

Notice these three things. It matters not what profession a man makes: if he does not hear the voice of the Son of God he is not a Christian, and therefore the Savior does not know him as His own. No matter what profession he may make, if he does not follow the Lord Jesus Christ he is only a sham and a fraud and a hypocrite. He may follow for a little while outwardly, like those of whom the Apostle Peter speaks who walk in the way of righteousness and then turn from it. "But it is happened unto them according to the true proverb, The dog is turned to his own vomit again; and the sow that was washed to her wallowing in the mire" (2 Peter 2:22). If that dog had ever been regenerated and become a sheep, if that sow had ever been changed and become a lamb, neither would have gone back to the filth; but, you see, the dog was always a dog, and the sow was always a sow. They were just whitewashed, not washed white; they were never regenerated, and so went back to the old things.

But the sheep of Christ are different. "They follow Me," Jesus says. Be careful. Do not profess to be one of His sheep if you do not follow Him. It is the test of reality. There are many people who tell us, "At such and such a time I was converted, I went forward, I signed a card." You can do all of these things and be lost forever. What you need is a new birth, and when you are born again, you get a new life; and when you receive a new life, you love to follow Jesus, and if you do not, you are not a Christian. Take that home. Examine your own foundations a bit.

A Dangerous Doctrine?

People say, "If you preach this doctrine of the eternal security of the believer, men will say, 'Well, then it doesn't make any difference what I do, I will get to heaven anyway.' " It makes a tremendous difference what you do. If you do not behave yourself, it shows that you are not a real Christian. I know that a real Christian may fail, but the difference can be seen in Peter and Judas. Peter failed, and failed terribly, but he was genuine, and one look from Jesus sent him out weeping bitterly; his heart was broken to think that he had so dishonored his Lord. But Judas companied with the Lord almost three and a half years and was a devil all the time; he was a thief and was seeking his own interest. He was even made the treasurer of that company, and he held the bag, but we read, "He bare away what was put therein" (John 12:6), as this has been literally translated. At last remorse overtook him, not genuine repentance, and what was the result? He went and hanged himself. He was never a child of God. There is a great difference, you see, between a Christian and a false professor.

Justified by Faith

"My sheep hear my voice, and I know them, and they follow me: and I give unto them eternal life." Do you believe it? I do not understand how people can read a passage like that and then talk about a Christian losing his life. It would not be eternal if it could be lost. "And they shall never perish, neither shall any man pluck them out of my hand." The original is very strong here. In the English a double negative makes an affirmative, but in Greek it only strengthens a declaration: "They shall never, no, never, perish."

It is impossible, it is unthinkable, that one who has eternal life shall ever perish. "My Father, which gave them me, is greater than all; and no man is able to pluck them out of my Father's hand." Here I am, a poor lost sinner, but the Lord in grace picks me up and saves me, and I am in His hand. And now the Father puts His hand around too, and I am in the hand of the Father and of the Son, and the Devil himself cannot get me unless he can loosen those hands.

Could you think of any greater security than to be in the hands of the Father and of the Son? "Never perish"—"eternal life"—what wondrous words are these! Do not be afraid of God's truth. You might as well be afraid of the beginning of the gospel that God can freely forgive and justify a guilty sinner by faith in the Lord Jesus Christ. People try to put guards around that truth and say, "Yes, you are justified by faith if you have enough good works to add to it." That is not true; it is by faith alone, and good works spring from that. When you know you have eternal life, you will find your heart so filled with love to Christ that you will try to live for His glory.

Objections

There will be certain passages coming up in the minds of different ones, and they will say, "What he has said may sound logical enough, but what about this Scripture and that?" Let me say, there is no possible Scripture that will come to your mind that the present speaker has not considered carefully over and over again. I have not time in one address to go into all these, but I can assure you that having examined them all with the greatest degree of care, I have never been able to find one that can set aside this: "Neither death, nor life, nor angels, nor principalities, nor powers, nor things present, nor things to come, nor height, nor depth, nor any other creature, shall be able to separate us from the love of God, which is in Christ Jesus our Lord."

If you have a clear, definite, positive Scripture, do not allow some passage that is perplexing, that is difficult of interpretation, that seems somewhat ambiguous, to keep you from believing the positive statement, "He that believeth hath everlasting life."

It is because I have a salvation like this to offer to men, it is because God has sent me to proclaim a salvation like this to sinners, that I have confidence in inviting people to come to Jesus, for I know if they get in living touch with my Savior He will make them His forever.

Donald Grey Barnhouse
1895-1960

Donald Grey Barnhouse had an effective thirty-three-year ministry at Tenth Presbyterian Church in Philadelphia as well as a radio ministry. He was director of the well-known Stony Brook School for Boys, editor of Revelation Magazine (Eternity) *from 1931 until 1960, and author of thirty books including* Teaching the Word of Truth.

"Your Right to Heaven" is one of the earlier sermons of Dr. Barnhouse. It was this message that sparked the basic approach for the Evangelism Explosion ministry in Fort Lauderdale, Florida.

Your Right
to Heaven

We are living in a day when everyone is demanding his rights. Labor pleads for the rights of the working man. Industry cries for its rights with equal vigor. The colored races demand equal rights with their white brethren. Oriental nations demand independence and national status. And some even are demanding the right to do as they please regardless of the cost to others.

Among the various rights of men and nations there is one which every man, woman and child must consider—the right to enter heaven. Have men a right to enter heaven? This question was anticipated many years ago by the Apostle Paul. In language clear and concise and unequivocal, the great apostle in his letter to the Romans states that no man on his record has any right whatsoever to enter heaven. In the third chapter of his epistle to the Romans, verses 19 and 20, he says, "Now we know that what things soever the law saith, it saith to them who are under the law; that every mouth may be stopped, and all the world may become guilty before God. Therefore, by the deeds of the law there shall no flesh be justified in his sight; for by the law is the knowledge of sin." In this passage Paul states that in the light of man's record and God's perfect standard, no man has a right to enter heaven.

When you first read this you may be shocked and insulted. But look for a moment at the answer of the apostle and you will see immediately that there can be no other answer. Put yourself in the role of a patient who comes to a doctor in order that you may know the state of your health. For just as a doctor has certain diagnostic questions that become almost routine for use with practically every patient, so there are spiritual diagnostic techniques. When a person comes with a problem, we proceed somewhat as follows:

"First of all, we must find out whether we are going to deal with your need as with the need of a believer in Christ or an unbeliever. Have you been born again?" If there is an immediate clear-cut testimony that shows an intelligent knowledge of redemption and a faith that is committed to Christ as Savior and Lord, the problem itself can be dealt with.

But if there is any hesitancy, any wavering, any doubt as to the questioner's personal salvation, we say, "Perhaps I can clarify your thinking with a question. You know that there are a great many accidents today. Suppose that you and I should go out of this building and a swerving automobile should come up on the sidewalk and kill the two of us. In the next moment we would be what men call dead. Now we brush aside as folly that we are going to meet St. Peter at any gate. How such nonsense exists outside of jokes is very difficult to comprehend. Christ says that He is the door; and there need be no keys to that door, for Christ also says: 'him that cometh to me I will in no wise cast out.' When the Lord Jesus Christ died on Calvary's cross and arose again from the dead, by that very act He opened the door of heaven and gave every man access to God through Himself. Christ is the *open* door, but He is also the *only* door. He says, 'I am the way, the truth, and the life: no man cometh unto the Father, but by me' (John 14:6).

"So the door to Heaven is opened wide, and when you die it is God Himself you must face. And if in this next minute He should say to you, 'What right do you have'—not 'why would you like to come'—'what right do you have to come into My heaven?' what would be your answer?"

Literally hundreds of people have had their thinking brought to clarity through following this line of thought. There are three possible answers, and it will be seen that our text comes into the picture in a commanding fashion.

The first answer will be variations on the theme of presenting one's life and works to the scrutiny of God and claiming that one has done the best that he could and that surely God would not be too hard on a sincere man who has plugged along without harming his neighbors too much. The variations are many, all the way from boasting to having lived always by the Golden Rule down to the statement that one has lived up to a certain code or that one has never been guilty of murder and the grosser sins.

Two particular conversations will illustrate phases of this attempt to present works to God as the price of entry into heaven. Early in my ministry I met a man casually who happened to live a few doors from the church. When I spoke to him about his soul, he laughed me off patronizingly, telling me that he was not the kind of man that needed the church or anything else. He was an active member of a lodge, he said, and if any man lived up to the high principles of that particular lodge, he would be all right.

I saw him from time to time, and whenever I attempted to speak to him about his soul he would tell me, once more, that he was living up to his lodge obligations. We are not speaking against lodges. If you want to drill and exchange passwords and handgrips, and if you want to have an insurance and benevolence scheme with some other men and women, go right ahead. But if you say you can go to heaven by living up to a society's obligations, you are desperately mistaken.

The sequel of the story will reveal the poverty of any such idea. The day came when this man was stricken with serious illness and was not expected to live out the day. I went to see him. A member of his lodge was already there on what they called the death-watch, so that no member of their group would have to die alone. This man was seated across the room from the bed, reading a magazine. I had scarcely entered the room when his successor came and the shift was changed, one man leaving and the other man taking his place. The man's case was desperate, and a desperate remedy was necessary.

Sitting down by the man's bedside, I said to him, "You do not mind my staying a few minutes and watching you, do you? I have wondered what it would mean to die without Christ, and I have known you for several years now as a man who said he did not need Christ but that his lodge obligations were enough, and I would like to see a man come to the end that way, to see what it is like."

He looked at me like a wounded animal and slowly said, "You . . . wouldn't . . . mock a . . . dying man . . . would you?" I then asked him what he would answer when God asked him what right he would have to enter the Lord's holy heaven. Great tears ran down the man's pale and wrinkled cheeks, and he looked at me in agonized silence. Then swiftly I told him how he might approach God through the merits of the Lord Jesus Christ, and it was not long before he began to say that his mother had taught him these things as a child, but that he had abandoned them. But in those moments he came back to God through Jesus Christ, and in a little while he had the members of his family called that they might hear his testimony of faith, and they heard him say that he wished that his story might be told at his funeral, which it was a few days later.

A second story illustrates the same point from another angle. A young officer of the United States Marines came to visit our church during the war. His brother was a believer, and the Marine was intrigued with the change that had come over his brother. When he was asked if he were saved, he wavered in his reply. Next came the diagnostic question: "What answer would you give if death claimed you and God should say to you, 'What right do you have to come into My heaven?'" He replied that he would say something like, "Well, God, there is the record of my life. I have never committed any great sins."

"Lieutenant, permit me to be very frank. If you dared attempt any such answer, you could never enter heaven." He broke in to say, "I have been giving much thought to these things recently, for we have been practicing crawling across a field under live ammunition bursts, and I have wondered what would happen to me if I humped too high." I replied, "Lieutenant, suppose you drove a car up the main street of your city at fifty miles an hour, through all the traffic lights, without any regard to the police whistles. Finally you are overtaken, and you reach out and slap the policeman. When they finally get you to court, they throw the book at you. The total of your fine is $300, and you have no money, but your brother pays your fine for you; and while he is doing it, you start for the door. A policeman says to you, 'What right do you have to leave the courtroom?' Note the phrase, what right? Would you say to him, 'Why, there's my record. I am the man who drove the car up the street at fifty miles an hour and slapped the policeman; so now let me go'?" He answered, "Of course not; I would say that my fine had been paid."

"Exactly! It is not your record that lets you go free; it is your record that brought you there in the first place. And if any man thinks he can arrive in heaven because of his record, he is not really thinking. It is his record that raises the question. If he had no record with sin in it, he could say, 'Move over, God, and let me sit down on the throne with You. I've arrived at last, and my record brought me in.'" The lieutenant shook his head, and said,

"Of course. I see it plainly now. It is not my record, but the fact that the Lord Jesus Christ paid my fine by dying on the cross." And thus another man passed out of death and into life.

On another occasion, several years before the recent war, we were crossing the Atlantic one summer and I was asked to preach at the Sunday service the second or third day out. After that there were several conversations about spiritual matters with people who came up to ask questions. One conversation was with a young woman who was a professor of languages in one of the Eastern colleges. The diagnostic question was asked: "If this ship should go to the bottom of the sea, and we were what men called dead, and God asked you: 'What right do you have to come into My heaven?' what would you say?"

She answered, "I wouldn't have a thing to say." I replied, "You are quoting Paul in Romans 3:19." She was puzzled and I said to her, "Can you recreate your answer, every syllable of it? I asked what you would say if God said, 'What right do you have to come into My heaven?' " She thought a moment, and then answered correctly, "Why, I said, I wouldn't have a thing to say."

I then opened the New Testament to the text I am discussing and made her read it. "Now we know that what things soever the law saith, it saith to them that are under the law; that every mouth may be stopped, and all the world may become guilty before God." When she had finished, I said, "What does it say? That every mouth may be . . ." And she read it slowly, " . . . stopped. That every mouth may be stopped." "That's right. You said it in American, 'I wouldn't have a thing to say.' God says that your mouth would be stopped. It is the same thing." And then I led her to see that there is another answer, a great and wonderful answer to the question.

Yes, there are only three possible answers. One: "There's my record." And this is an answer that exists only in present imagination but which would never reach the lips when folly has been put by and men stand in the clear light of truth without excuse. Two: "I wouldn't have a thing to say." And that is the horrible truth; for speechless you would confront the Savior whom you had trampled in your neglect, and who now would have become your outraged Judge. The men who pause briefly at the judgment-bar of God before going to their eternal doom will never open their lips in their own defense. They will know then that they have no defense, and that they are indeed without excuse.

If there is a word spoken at the judgment-bar of God by human beings who are being sent to their place in outer darkness, it will be that which is forced from their reluctant lips by an all-powerful God. They will cry, "It was all true, O God. I was wrong. I knew I was wrong when I made my excuses. But I hated and I still hate righteousness by the blood of Christ. I must admit that those despised Christians were right who bowed before Thee and acknowledged their dependence upon Thee. I hated their songs of faith then, and I hate them now. They were right, and I hated them because they were right and because they belonged to Thee, and I hate them now because they belong to Thee. I wanted my own way. And I still want my own way. I want heaven, but I want heaven without Thee. I want heaven with myself on the throne. That's what I want and I do not want anything else, and never, never will I want anything other than heaven with myself on the throne. I want my way. And now I am going to the place of desire without fulfillment, of lust without satisfaction, of wanting without having, of wishing but never getting, of looking but never seeing, and I hate, I hate, I hate, because I want my own way. I hate Thee, O God, for not letting me have my way. I hate, I hate . . ." And their voices will drift off to utter nothingness moaning, "I hate . . ."

And though there may be such a chorus of the damned, there will never be a word allowed in self-defense. They will see truth by the light of truth and will attempt subterfuge no more. Every mouth will be stopped along that line.

Will you sing this chorus of hate? Will you be a member of the chorale of the damned? You need not be. You can in no wise present your record as a right to enter heaven, and perhaps you too are in the position of the teacher who said, "I haven't a thing to say," for your mouth is stopped and will be stopped on that great day of judgment.

But there is a wonderful answer because the same apostle that wrote these terrible words, pointing out to us that our record is not satisfactory to God, also has set forth God's wonderful provision. For we read a few verses further on, "Being justified freely by his grace through the redemption that is in Christ Jesus: whom God has set forth to be a propitiation through faith in his blood, to declare his righteousness for the remission of sins that are past, through the forebearance of God; to declare, I say, at this time his righteousness: that he might be just, and the justifier of him which believeth in Jesus" (Romans 3:24-26). This is the answer. This gives us the right to enter heaven.

> Nothing in my hands I bring,
> Simply to Thy cross I cling.
> All for sin could not atone,
> Thou must save and Thou alone.

> Rock of ages cleft for me,
> Let me hide myself in Thee.

This is your only plea. This is your only right to enter heaven. Accept the Lord Jesus Christ as your own personal Savior, and come to know the assurance and peace which He gives.

> The holy, meek, unspotted Lamb,
> Who from the Father's bosom came,
> Who died for me, even me, to atone,
> Now for my Lord, and God, I own.

> When from the dust of death I rise
> To claim my mansion in the skies,
> Even then this shall be all my plea—
> Jesus hath lived, hath died for me!

> Ah! give to all Thy servants, Lord,
> With power to speak Thy gracious Word,
> That all who to Thy wounds will flee,
> May find eternal life in Thee.

The Lord Jesus Christ has said: "Verily, verily I say unto you, he that heareth my word and believeth on him that sent me, hath everlasting life, and shall not come into condemnation, but is passed from death unto life" (John 5:24).

James McGinlay
1901-1958

James McGinlay was a Scottish-born pastor-evangelist of exceptional ability. He held pastorates in Canada and the United States and was much in demand as a Bible conference speaker. Foremost as a sermon stylist, his every message was spiced with humor and was a practical answer and challenge to the problems of the day. His dynamic preaching and his faculty to intelligently and uncompromisingly present the gospel message stirred entire congregations and communities.

"The Birthday of Souls" is a sample of his preaching style.

The Birthday
of Souls

Isaiah 66: 7, 8

Before she travailed, she brought forth; before her pain came she was delivered of a man child. Who hath heard of such a thing? Who hath seen such things? Shall the earth be made to bring forth in one day? Or shall a nation be born at once? For as soon as Zion travailed, she brought forth her children.

As a minister of the gospel, I have sometimes wished that God's ways were my ways, and His thoughts mine, so that by a process of mental reasoning I could explain to myself and to others some mysteries associated with the salvation of the lost. We are all agreed that nothing but the Word of God, energized by the Spirit of God, will ever save a sinner from the error of his ways. No mystery about that, is there?

Yet before sinners are stirred, God Himself must be moved, and apparently the only power that can perform this colossal task is the prayers of the Lord's own people. Why doesn't the omnipotent God save souls without our prayers and apart from our preaching? Why doesn't He gather into His Kingdom the heathen from Africa, India, China, and Japan, independently of human help? God knows the tragic record of our frailty; He is not ignorant concerning the true state of our lives, for our sin of commission and omission has long provided Him with food for bitter grief.

Notwithstanding, it is perfectly obvious that God has no intention of saving sinners unless and until we do our part. Please do not go to sleep now, or permit your interest in this message to lag, upon the assumption that the speaker is heretical concerning the sovereignty of God. On the contrary, I believe that God is the author and finisher of salvation, and upon His deserving brow I place the crown of laurels, giving all honor and glory to Him for our redemption.

Not for one minute must we relegate to any but the power of Christ's Word the credit for raising dead Lazarus from the grave. But before our Savior cried, "Lazarus, come forth," He said to His disciples, "Take ye away the stone." Divinity and humanity must needs work together before the blinds are pulled up and the grief dispelled from the little home of Martha and Mary in Bethany. Cornelius, the centurion of Bible fame, was a very devout man as naturally devout men go. In fact, an angelic visitation was the great distinction he and his family enjoyed. Have any celestial messengers been around your home lately? Likely not, but they did patronize the house of an unregenerate Caesarean. Before this Roman gentleman could become a Christian, it was necessary for Peter to deliver in his presence the gospel message setting forth the saving grace of God. Prior to this, however, our Heavenly Father had to deal with stubborn Peter. It always puzzles me to figure out why an all-powerful God, who could lower a tray of meats from the sky as an object lesson to a thick-headed saint, could not by direct interposition save a tender-hearted sinner. But no, here we are again confronted with the eternal enigma of human and divine cooperation.

Please do not ask, "Couldn't God save Cornelius without the help of Peter?" My business is not to explain what God couldn't do, but declare what He did. If perchance I were successful in clearing up the case of Cornelius, my next problem would be to tackle the case of the Ethiopian whose conversion apparently could not be consummated until Philip the evangelist was caught away from a revival in Samaria to interpret Isaiah 53 to a lone sinner in the desert.

May God help us to believe that when we get to heaven, in all probability we shall discover very few glorified saints whose conversion on earth was entirely divorced from some human influence.

The Mistaken Conception of Revival

Prevalent among many churches today is an erroneous idea concerning the true meaning of revival. Months ahead they locate some noted evangelist and then "hook him for a Fall campaign."

They imagine that if during the interim between the setting of the date and the actual commencement of the meetings no outrageous sin disgraces their profession, upon the first night of the expert's endeavor a mighty revival will fall, either from heaven or down his coat sleeves—they know not, nor do they care just so long as "IT" comes. When the meetings are over and the meagre results tabulated, the more sanguine of the flock who really expected a catch of one hundred and fifty and three shake their disappointed heads and say to one another, "Well, that evangelist *humor* is like the old grey mare—he ain't what he used to be." The other crowd who really never did want the meetings, but merely voted in favor of them to preserve the unanimity of the fold are perfectly delighted with the results. With a gleam in their eye that bespeaks satisfaction, they say to the poor discouraged preacher (who by this time is praying for a new church), "Well, Pastor, it is *humor* just as we expected."

Strangely enough, however, the same evangelist leaves that place, goes to another, preaches the same sermons, and the windows of heaven are opened and the blessing of God falls—the saints are revived and sinners are converted. Why the difference? The text explains it. There was little or no concern for the lost in the first assembly. Strife, envy, jealousy, and worldliness were the order of the day. In such places it would be extremely difficult for either Michael or Gabriel from heaven to make much progress and produce satisfactory results.

In the second church there was a spirit of prayer. The saints were burdened for the lost. The dearth of conversions had saddened them and impelled them to cry, "O God, how long, how long?" Mothers and fathers were weeping on account of their wayward sons. "And as soon as Zion travailed she brought forth *Isaiah 66* her children."

Yes, just as a mother goes down into the valley of the shadow *baby* of death, giving birth to her child, so must the church collectively, and the saints individually, travail in spirit before sinners will be born into the Kingdom of God. You may send a mother to the hospital, place her under the care of the most expert obstetrician, but it is not until she travails that the babe is born. The Spirit of God penned our text not for the purpose of being vulgar, but in order that we might perceive the striking analogy between the physical and the spiritual. If we would see our loved ones saved, and our churches transformed from religious morgues into spiri-

73

tual maternity wards, we must be willing, for Jesus' sake, to pay the price.

Biblical and Historical Examples of Travail

As we study the Word of God, and the sacred and secular records of the church's career, we can do not else but admit that travail was always prerequisite to revival. When Nehemiah in Shushan the palace was informed by Hanani and certain men of Judah that the remnant were in great affliction and the walls of Jerusalem razed to the ground, he sat down and wept and mourned certain days, and fasted, and prayed before the God of heaven. Listen to his plea.

> I beseech thee, O Lord God of Heaven, the great and terrible God, that keepeth covenant and mercy for them that love him and observe his commandments: Let thine ear now be attentive, and thine eyes open, that thou mayest hear the prayer of thy servant, which I pray before thee now, day and night, for the children of Israel thy servants, and confess the sins of the children of Israel, which we have sinned against thee: both I and my father's house have sinned. (Nehemiah 1:5, 6)

Before the walls were rebuilt and the people blest, somebody had to pray night and day.

In the book of Esther, the noble yet comparatively obscure Mordecai was the man behind the scenes who wrought deliverance for the Jews. The intervention of Esther within the palace gates would have proven futile apart from the divine reinforcement supplied by her foster-father's prayers without.

> When Mordecai perceived all that was done, he rent his clothes and put on sackcloth and ashes, and went down into the midst of the City and cried with a loud and bitter cry. (Esther 4:1)

Jeremiah, the weeping prophet, is illustrative of our text. He cried, "My bowels, my bowels, I am pained at my heart because they have forsaken thy law" (Jeremiah 4:19). Look at Daniel. He prayed twenty-one days and did not cease till he had obtained the blessing. He sought it by prayer and supplications, with fasting, sackcloth, and ashes; and after he held on for three weeks the answer came. Why didn't the answer come sooner? God sent an archangel to bear the message, but the Devil hindered him (Daniel 10:11-14).

Peter is given great credit for the conversion of three thousand souls on the day of Pentecost. God bless him, he is the last man in heaven from whom I would subtract one ounce of glory. Yet we must remember that one hundred and twenty had travailed in the upper room, and on the morning when the first church walked down the stairs to be given life at Pentecost, they were in a God-conscious frame of mind and attitude of heart. It is comparatively easy to be a Holy Ghost preacher if one is privileged to minister the Word of Truth to a Holy Ghost people. It *quote* has been said that the pew will rise no higher than the pulpit, in which assertion I concur; but God help the poor pulpit in a church whose pews are spiritually down in the cellar.

Martin Luther could never have rocked the Vatican, nor shook the world for God had it not been for the humble saints in the forests of Germany, in the dungeons of Spain, in the fields of England, and on the hills of Scotland who were crying out night and day to God for deliverance from the bloody tyranny of the ecclesiastical harlot: "Shall not God avenge His own elect, which cry day and night unto Him" (Luke 18:7). He did.

Next to reading the Bible itself, I recommend as a tonic for your soul a study of the biographies of men who were luminaries in the realm of evangelism. Of Finney's power in prayer, one of the early students at Oberlin said, "The Class in Theology of 1838 met to hear one of the last lectures of the course. Finney as usual knelt with us in offering the opening prayer, but the burden on his soul for us, for Zion, and for the lost world could not be thrown off in a few petitions. For a whole hour he led us up to God. We then arose and went in profound silence to our rooms. There was no lecture that day. His prayer we can never forget."

Would God we had some colleges today in the world whose presidents or professors would storm the Throne of Heaven in prayer for one hour instead of utilizing that valuable time at their disposal explaining away the faith of Finney and other intellectual giants who had tapped the spiritual resources of heaven and turned thousands to God. Whitefield, Jonathan Edwards, and others ofttimes spent whole nights in prayer travailing for souls; and just as surely as they preached next day, so did God save sinners.

Have We a Concern for the Lost Souls?

On every hand today we hear that the imminency of the Lord's return makes the wholesale conversion of sinners not only improbable but impossible. The day of revival is over; therefore, we need not expect to witness any great stir among the unregenerate. Well, my friends, if you have a loved one out of Christ, on his or her way to hell, I beg of you to remember that God has not changed, the gospel has not changed, the Holy Ghost has not changed, and even in this apostate day our Heavenly Father hath no pleasure in the death of the wicked.

If the people of God, instead of running around with a prophetic telescope to their eyes looking for the anti-Christ, and the man of sin, and the geographical location for the battle of Armageddon, were travailing for souls, revival instead of dry rot would be the prevailing order in many of our good orthodox churches. I believe in the rapture of the saints and kindred truths associated therewith, but while my heart is crying, "Even so, Lord Jesus, come quickly," my lips are warning sinners to flee from the wrath to come.

Do you mothers and fathers ever weep on behalf of your children who are perishing? Do you wives send up a heart-rending cry to God to save your husbands from hell? If they pay no attention to the preacher's sermons, maybe they will to your tears. Reveal by your grief that sorrow has possessed your heart on account of their precarious condition. If they ask why you are sad, tell them that it almost breaks your heart to think that while you and the redeemed are enjoying the eternal felicity of heaven, they will be enduring the everlasting misery of hell. If Christ in lonely Gethsemane at midnight was in such travail of soul for lost men that "His sweat was as it were great drops of blood falling down to the ground," how in God's name do we expect sinners to be saved until we at least approximate a little of His anxiety?

I have a friend who over a period of years prayed for and pleaded with his unsaved brother. As time went on, the object of his concern exhibited less and less interest in Christ, and became more vehement in his determination to reject Him. My friend said to me in a somewhat exasperated tone of voice, "Never have I pleaded with a harder case. Talking to my brother about things eternal is like casting one's pearls before swine. He does everything in defiance against God, and for the life of me I see no hope."

Apparently he had communicated this pessimism to his mother in England, for one day he showed me a letter which he had received from her hand. Concerning her unsaved son she said to my friend, "Don't worry about Reg. I prayed the rest of you into the Kingdom, and so will I do with him." We both admired the faith of this old soul, and agreed that she was so typically motherly in her faith that God would one day save her prodigal.

Some months later another brother, a Christian and a deacon in a little church in British Columbia, was sitting in his usual pew worshiping God with the rest of the congregation. Suddenly the door opened, and to his utter amazement in walked this unsaved man. Without waiting for sermon or invitation from the pulpit, he made his way to the front, motioned to the preacher, and said, "Tell me, sir, what must I do to be saved? I can stand this no longer and have come from the ranch in the mountains this morning to find God. Can you help me?"

Ah, what was the explanation? Several thousands of miles away in a little home across the sea, a mother who believed God and loved her son's soul was beseeching the Throne of Grace on his behalf. In answer to her prayer, the omnipresent Holy Spirit invaded that lonely house in the British Columbian hills, apprehended the sinner who was apparently across the dead line, and that Sabbath morning impelled him to travel to a place of worship where he might be pointed "to the Lamb of God that taketh away the sin of the world."

Imagine having souls saved before the choir sings its anthem? Imagine having sinners converted before the preacher even announces the text? Yet, that is what we could have, and what we would have, if people today were really burdened for the lost. You go to church on a Sunday after a week of travailing for sinners and communing with God on their behalf, and I tell you, brethren, you won't care whether the sermon to which you listen with interest has a first point, second point, third point, or conclusion;

ILLUSTRATION STORY

whether the text is from the Old Testament or the New; high doctrine or low. Your concern will be for human derelicts, and your ambition to see them saved.

Isaiah 66

"As soon as Zion travailed she brought forth."

The Effect of Travail for the Lost

The day is too far spent for us to idle away our time in useless speculation as to whether it is necessary for Christians to travail before God will save souls. I pray that the message thus far has clarified your mind concerning this truth. However, a perfectly legitimate question might be, of what value is travail to the Christian? If God could by His sovereign power save sinners without our aid, then surely the inclusion of human cooperation must be for a purpose beneficial to us.

Even in the physical realm, "We are not skilled to understand what God hath willed, what God has planned," and among the *baby* mysteries of life is the vicarious suffering of a mother before her firstborn is brought into the world. Although we cannot explain why she should go through the valley of the shadow of death in giving birth to her child, yet we must admit that her travail has a tremendous effect upon her love for that baby afterward. We are all agreed that there is a vast difference in the quality of maternal and paternal affection. In fact, the nearest approach to the incomparable love of God for sinners is the love of a mother for her offspring.

We fathers love our children, but the more truthful among us must admit that when the baby has whooping cough, colic, or croup at 3 o'clock on a cold wintry morning, the mother's love travels further and faster than ours. Mother is usually at the little sufferer's side relieving his distress before tender-hearted father has convinced himself that the little fellow is ever in need. The child is more precious to the one who suffered most to give it life, and even when a grown-up prodigal breaks the parents' hearts, the mother never forgets that the son now behind prison bars is the baby for whom she tasted death.

If God were to save souls in churches whose members had never suffered or sacrificed on behalf of sinners, how much, or rather how little, genuine affection would be lavished upon that babe in Christ after his conversion. "God loves a world of sinners lost, and ruined by the Fall," because He Himself suffered, bled, and died to save their souls from hell. Our Father has no desire to save souls in a church where His converts would be treated as orphans or stepchildren, of the unfortunate type whose little hearts pine for love and seldom receive it. Therefore, the Bible has decreed that we travail before their conversion, so that we shall care for them afterward.

Lord, speak to me, that I may speak,
In living echoes of Thy tone;
As Thou hast sought, so let me seek
Thy erring children lost and lone.

Oh, lead me, Lord, that I may lead
The wandering and the wavering feet!
Oh, feed me, Lord, that I may feed
Thy hungering ones with manna sweet!

Oh, strengthen me, that while I stand
Firm on the Rock, and strong in Thee,
I may stretch out a loving hand
To wrestlers with the troubled sea.

John R. Rice
1895-1980

John R. Rice was one of the great evangelists of our day. He was known as "America's dean of evangelists" and was sometimes called "Will Rogers of the pulpit." His ministry was colorful and controversial because of his intense stand against modernism and infidelity and his fight for the fundamentals.

Dr. Rice wrote more than two hundred titles with a circulation of sixty-one million copies. Through October 1981 a total of 24,058 souls reported accepting Christ through his ministries, not counting those saved in his crusades or in countries overseas where his literature has been translated.

His sermons were sensational, spectacular—but Scriptural. He preached against sin, on the home, godly Christian living, prayer, revival, and prophecy.

Dr. Rice's book Prayer—Asking and Receiving is considered a Christian classic. His gospel tract "What Must I Do to Be Saved?" has been printed in thirty-nine languages, and distribution has reached into the millions.

The following sermon was one of Dr. Rice's favorites.

When God's Patience Wears Out!

And the Lord said, My Spirit shall not always strive with man. (Genesis 6:3)

Little is said in the pulpits these days about the time when God's patience comes to an end, but that theme is often discussed in Scripture.

The destruction of the entire race, saving Noah and his family—eight souls in all, was because God grew impatient with man's insatiable, unending wickedness.

God set a time limit on His mercy! He deliberately warned that His Spirit would not continue indefinitely striving, warning, pleading with the wicked. After one hundred and twenty years there was to come God's horrible judgment in the destruction of the entire race, saving the family in the Ark.

Read the background for the subject in Genesis 6:3-8:

"And the Lord said, My Spirit shall not always strive with man, for that he also is flesh: yet his days shall be an hundred and twenty years.

"There were giants in the earth in those days; and also after that, when the sons of God came in unto the daughters of men, and they bare children to them, the same became mighty men which were of old, men of renown.

"And God saw that the wickedness of man was great in the earth, and that every imagination of the thoughts of his heart was only evil continually.

"And it repented the Lord that he had made man on the earth, and it grieved him at his heart.

"And the Lord said, I will destroy man whom I have created from the face of the earth; both man, and beast, and the creeping thing, and the fowls of the air; for it repenteth me that I have made them.

"But Noah found grace in the eyes of the Lord."

God is the unchanging God: "For I am the Lord, I change not" (Malachi 3:6); "Jesus Christ the same yesterday, and today, and forever" (Hebrews 13:8). His attitude toward sin is the same today as it was in the days of Noah, before the Flood. There is a limit to God's patience. His Spirit will not always strive with men.

God's Holy Spirit Does Strive

God seeking men! God pleading with men! How foolish the idea of the modernist that man is always seeking God, always climbing toward God! The contrary teaching of the Bible and experience is that men are aliens from God, oppose God, rebel against God, and that those who are saved are won only by the long seeking, pleading, and striving of the Spirit.

In the cool of the day God walked in the Garden and called for Adam. "Where art thou?" Before the Flood, when God saw that man's wickedness was so great that "every imagination of the thoughts of his heart was only evil continually," still the Spirit warned and pleaded and knocked at the door of every heart among those violent, licentious, and rebellious men!

Today the Holy Spirit still calls every sinner. Not one dies unconverted and goes to the place of torment but that first he was warned, intreated to turn to God. How tenderly the blessed Spirit strives with sinners!

Let us remember that people are not saved by preaching of itself; they are only saved by such preaching as that which has upon it the breath of God, the moving of the Spirit. Even the Word of God can only be the instrument of salvation as the Spirit takes it to men's hearts.

How fruitless, how powerless, is all the preaching, all the testimony which is not moving, pleading, warning and the invitation of the Spirit Himself!

Men are saved because they are called by the Holy Spirit. It is not the letter of the Word that saves. Many preachers who quote much Scripture are utterly powerless. The Word is "the sword of the Spirit," and if the Spirit does not wield His own sword, it does not cut. But the Spirit seeks, convicts, warns, and strives with the lost to be saved.

How infinitely multiplied is God's mercy! He seeks men, runs after them, strives with them to be saved. Men insult God and blaspheme His holy name; yet His Spirit continues to strive with sinners. Men go on in their drunkenness and licentiousness and in every other form of degrading sin; still the Spirit pleads. They may even deny the fact of God, may loudly proclaim they are agnostics or atheists; yet God's Spirit still calls, still loves, still woos. Men may be long convicted and fight against God for years; yet the Spirit often continues His warning and convicting and calling.

Though I was saved at about nine years of age, still I remember a series of incidents through which God spoke to my heart and convicted me.

At about four, I was taught in Sunday school about the baby Jesus and how He had to be born in an old stable because they had no room for Him in the inn. I kept that little picture Sunday school card given me that day and felt guilty in my own heart that people like me had no room for Jesus.

When I was about five I was deeply moved by a song my mother sang, "Turned Away from the Beautiful Gate." Even then I seemed to know that it was by their own sinful rebellion and rejection of Christ that people missed heaven. I remember my unrest of soul.

About the same time, when I told my mother a lie she explained how God hated lies and what a sin a lie was. The occasion was burned on my memory. I felt I deserved the condemnation of God. Surely that was God speaking to me through His Spirit.

When Mother lay on her deathbed she talked of the Savior and had all of us promise to meet her in heaven. I felt myself under the spell of her dying smile and testimony until I trusted Christ.

After Mother's death, I remembered the tears and exhortations of my Sunday school teacher; the godly pastor telling the story of the prodigal son and how he himself had once been a prodigal, how he had run away from home and came to want and trouble, and how he was forgiven upon his return.

It seems God must have been calling me from the first day I knew about good and bad, from the first time I ever had a sense of moral responsibility to God!

Oh, the infinite mercy of God's Spirit who strives with us lest we should go to hell! What condescension! What long-continued mercy! Nearly every person who was ever saved can testify that long before he heeded God's call, he was dealt with by the Spirit which strove with his soul, warning and urging him to be saved.

The Holy Spirit moves the conscience, causing it to become more active. The Holy Spirit calls attention to accidents and deaths around us. When in danger, how many soldiers prayed who had never prayed before! The Holy Spirit calls attention to danger and to the need for forgiveness and salvation. He may use the simplest statement of a wife or mother, or the words of a hymn, to convict and save.

Certain physical manifestations often appear when a sinner is convicted by the Spirit. He brings tears to the sinner's eyes, causes quivering lips or a throbbing in the throat. When manifestly the Spirit was striving with sinners, many times I have seen them break out in a profuse sweat. Twice I have known men under deep conviction to faint or to lose consciousness. One such was a drunkard at Pacific Garden Mission in Chicago who said he had tried everything else and this was his last chance to escape slavery and eternal ruin; the other was a man in a great revival in Binghamton, New York, whom I will mention later.

One with whom the Spirit is striving may become violently angry or abusive. When approached by a personal worker in a revival service many years ago, my father left the church in anger, swearing he would never enter its doors again. But that night he found no sleep. The next morning a humble but now rejoicing believer sat on the same church steps waiting for the janitor to open up for a sunrise prayer meeting!

How foolish for a Christian to be offended or discouraged with such a sinner as long as the Spirit still strives with him! Rather, we should be bold and press the attack if the Spirit leads, then gratefully look forward to blessing as He works.

The fact that the Spirit does strive with sinners is a wonderful mark of God's mercy and the only hope of those who would not seek if they were not first sought by the Spirit.

It does not seem strange that God's patience wears out. It does not seem strange that He sent a flood when "God saw the wickedness of man was great in the earth, and that every imagination of the thoughts of his heart was only evil continually." It was not only that their wickedness was great in outward action, but men were wicked in the heart, in their imagination—"*every* imagination of the thoughts of his heart" was evil; every thought, imagination, dream, and idea "was *only* evil continually."

How wicked was the race of fallen men! So God said, "My Spirit shall not always strive with man, for that he also is flesh: yet his days shall be an hundred and twenty years" (Genesis 6:3).

It is not strange that God at last turned from mercy to judgment. It is not strange that He decided to bring His pleading, His striving with hearts of men to an end. It is not strange that His blessed Spirit should give those men up to their sins. Rather, the strange thing, the remarkable thing is that the Holy Spirit continued to plead for another one hundred and twenty years after the race was debased beyond hope of redemption, with the exception of Noah and his family. God's Spirit does strive with man.

But God's Patience Does Wear Out

At long last the Ark was finished. At twenty-three or twenty-four inches to a cubit, it was about six hundred feet long, one hundred feet wide, sixty feet high, with three stories. The boat had ocean-liner proportions and was equipped to carry two of every kind of beast, with seven of every clean beast, and enough food for both men and animals. It took one hundred and twenty years to prepare. All that time Noah was a preacher of righteousness. All that time the Spirit was speaking to hearts, striving with and urging men to turn to God.

For one hundred and twenty years the population in Noah's country heard the ring of the hammers and saw the big boat take form. Hundreds must have been busy felling trees, dressing the timbers, and collecting food for man and grain and hay for animals. No doubt the news of "Noah's folly" in that one hundred and twenty years went wherever man had wandered before the Flood. Millions knew about "Noahs' Ark" and about his preaching; they laughed at his warnings, at Noah's God!

I think the correct meaning of 1 Peter 3:18 and 19 is that by the Spirit Christ preached to those spirits now in prison—did it when God's Spirit was striving with men in Noah's day. Christ preached to them through the Spirit, by the mouth of Noah, before they died. Christ was preaching to them when Noah preached.

85

But when the one hundred and twenty years were over, God's patience ended. It is not that He suddenly lost His temper, not that He did not have enough grace under special temptation—no, no! But the time came when to withhold judgment any longer would be a sin, and a just and holy God could not sin. After long emphasis on mercy, the time came when God must put emphasis on righteousness. The time came when He must show His holiness, as He had shown His love.

Now God said to Noah, "Come thou and all thy house into the ark" (Genesis 7:1). Noah was given seven days' notice. The activity must have been like a gigantic circus preparing for an ocean voyage!

When all were in the Ark—Noah and Mrs. Noah, their sons and their wives, all the beasts and fowls that God had walk up the gangplank—God Himself shut the door! Then the fountains of the deep were opened, and the windows of heaven poured out floods of water.

Forty days and nights it rained. Soon the lowlands, then the hills were covered. I can imagine the screaming and hammering on the sides of the Ark of those wanting inside. But God had shut the door. God's patience had come to an end. Every trapped family now knew it was the act of an impatient God. Those swept from rooftops, those who ran across the plains trying to outrun the wall of floodwaters, knew when they were overwhelmed by the turgid, swirling waters that God's wrath had at last struck. Every fear-frenzied woman who prayed and cried as she scratched at the giant beams and planks of the Ark when it began to float, now ignored by the God who had shut up heaven against the prayers of wicked men, the God who had withdrawn His Spirit, knew that at last God's patience had worn out!

In Genesis 15:16 the Lord told Abraham that "the inquity of the Amorites is not yet full." Abraham could not yet take the land of the Amorites. Though they were idolaters and had earned the wrath of God, they had not yet reached the limit which God in wisdom and mercy had set. When they crossed that line, He would then decree their uttermost destruction.

Four hundred years pass. The children of Israel are brought out of Egypt and back into the land promised to Abraham. And in Deuteronomy 20:16 and 17 we have the startling command of God:

"But of the cities of these people, which the Lord thy God

doth give thee for an inheritance, thou shalt save alive nothing that breatheth: But thou shalt utterly destroy them; namely . . . the Amorites. . . ."

After infinite patience and mercy, after long struggling and pleading by the Spirit with an idolatrous people, God's patience wears out! Now He decrees the utter destruction of every man, woman, and child.

God has said, "My Spirit shall not always strive with man."

With the children of Israel, God exhibited matchless patience. Through the centuries He sent prophets to warn them. At last the northern kingdom was sent into captivity. Then long later the southern kingdom of Judah wore out God's patience. God called for Nebuchadnezzar to surround and take the city. Women ate their own children in this time of famine. After a terrible slaughter, the city was taken. The king's eyes were put out and his children slain. The remnant of people, all but the very poorest, were chained and carried captive to Babylon. The Temple was stripped of its gold and silver to the value of millions of dollars, then burned. Jerusalem was now a desolate city.

But God was patient. After seventy years the remnant went back to Jerusalem and under Ezra, then Nehemiah rebuilt the wall. Later the Temple was rebuilt. Now Jews of all the tribes had a homeland!

The Savior came. God sent His virgin-born Son. Officially the Jews despised and rejected Him. The Savior was put to death. Stephen was stoned. James was beheaded. Christians were scattered. But the long, unheeded warning of the Savior come to pass.

In 70 A.D. Titus, the Roman general, besieged and took that wicked and rebellious city. The golden candlestick and other sacred furniture of the Temple were carried to Rome. The Temple was burned to the ground—not one stone was left upon another, even as Jesus had foretold! According to Josephus, over a million people were killed in the siege. The remnant was sold as slaves, until Jewish slaves became a drag on the market and buyers could not be found. Ever since that time, the land has been trodden underfoot of the Gentiles and will continue to be until the "times of the Gentiles be fulfilled" (Luke 21:20-24). A horrible blindness came over the whole Jewish race (Romans 11:25). God's patience with Israel wore out.

Do not misunderstand me: God still has plans for His chosen

people, the Jews, and He will keep every promise He made to them. Enemies of Israel are under the curse of God. Hitler did Satan's horrible business. But out of every concentration camp, out of every overrun country where Jews and others have suffered, comes this lesson to us: *God's patience does wear out.* His Spirit shall not always strive with man. Romans 11:26, along with many other Scriptures, tells of the time when the eyes of the blinded Jews will be opened and a nation will be converted in a day. Oh, may God speed the time! But let every Gentile take warning, let every Christ-rejecter be solemnly reminded: God's Spirit will not always strive with man.

Down in Egypt God sent Moses to Pharaoh with this message: "Let my people go" (Exodus 8:1). You know the story, and how the plagues came on Egypt—water turned to blood; frogs in the dough-pans and in the beds; torment of flies; the irresistible hail destroying everything alive that was not protected; the lice; the diseases; the impenetrable darkness; and finally the midnight cry and the death of the firstborn in every family where there was no blood on the door when the Death Angel passed over. You can read all about it in Exodus, chapters 5 through 12. See how Pharaoh dilly-dallied; how he begged for temporary respite but had no genuine repentance; how he was willing for the Israelites to worship God, but only in the land; how the men were permitted to go only a little way, while women and children were to be left behind—then later, after further punishment, how women and children could go as well as the men, but all cattle were to be left behind. We are told again and again that Pharaoh hardened his heart, and how God hardened Pharaoh's heart too. God had been kind to Pharaoh, but His patience was running out.

At last the children of Israel left the land of bondage, after eating the Passover lamb, with staves in their hands and their loins girded. Pharaoh gathered his army and pursued the fleeing people. When the children of Israel were in the midst of the Red Sea, God told Moses to stretch out his hand which held the rod of God. When he did, the mighty waters, released from their invisible restraint, crashed together, covering Pharaoh and his army, utterly destroying them all, while Moses and his people walked safely through. As Pharaoh strangled in the waters, he surely must have remembered that God's patience does not go on forever.

God had plainly said, "My Spirit shall not always strive with man."

God Sometimes Withdraws
His Spirit from Striving with Sinners

As God deals with nations, so He deals with individuals in that His mercy, long scorned and rejected, is followed by judgment.

God's Spirit, no doubt, had dealt with every individual who died in the Flood. In each case they had adequate warning; in each case they rejected the strivings of the Spirit. It was to individuals that God said, "My Spirit shall not always strive with man."

When the Holy Spirit ceases to strive with a lost sinner, when the Holy Spirit does not call, does not plead, does not convict, then that sinner is lost forever and beyond any hope of salvation.

This means there is an unpardonable sin, a sin that has no forgiveness. Jesus said in Matthew 12:31, 32:

"Wherefore I say unto you, All manner of sin and blasphemy shall be forgiven unto men: but the blasphemy against the Holy Spirit shall not be forgiven unto men. And whosoever speaketh a word against the Son of man, it shall be forgiven him: but whosoever speaketh against the Holy Ghost, it shall not be forgiven him, neither in this world, neither in the world to come."

Note that when this talks about the unpardonable sin that has no forgiveness, it is not talking *about* the Holy Spirit. It is not simply ascribing the works of the Spirit to Satan. The unpardonable sin is deeper than that. It is a personal resistance against the Spirit, a blasphemous attitude toward the Spirit Himself that so grieves Him as to drive Him away so that He no longer struggles with a sinner, nor warns, nor convicts.

Some modern theologians have invented the idea, unheard of by our fathers, that no longer can one commit the unpardonable sin. But I make bold to say that God still declares, "My Spirit shall not always strive with man." God has not changed. His wrath has not changed. His mercy still wears out.

I can show you in a moment that men will continue to commit the unpardonable sin.

In Revelation 13:8 we are told, "And all that dwell upon the earth shall worship him [the man of sin, the Antichrist, the

Beast], whose names are not written in the book of life of the Lamb slain from the foundation of the world." It is clear that all who worship the Beast forever miss their chance of salvation. Their names are not written in the Book of Life. Revelation 14:10 and 11 says that all who worship the Beast and take his mark shall be tormented in hell. The time mentioned here is the future Great Tribulation when the Man of Sin or that great dictator, "the Beast," the Antichrist, shall appear. Millions will then commit the unpardonable sin. Those who take the mark of the Beast can never be saved, can never be forgiven; hence it is clear they will have committed the unpardonable sin.

Hebrews 6:4-6 says that if certain people, those who have been greatly enlightened and convicted concerning Christ, fall away from this conviction and enlightenment, then they can never be saved. It is impossible "to renew them again unto repentance; seeing they crucify to themselves the Son of God afresh, and put him to an open shame." Such people can never be brought back to the place where they might repent. This is the unpardonable sin. This is long after the personal ministry of Christ. And the context, especially verse 9 in the same chapter, shows that God is not talking about the backsliding Christians but about the unpardonable sin of lost people. They still do commit the unpardonable sin.

Does not the Holy Spirit convict sinners today as He did in Bible times? Do not sinners resist the Spirit or ignore His pleadings now as then? Sometimes there comes a crisis when a lost man must say "yes" or "no," when he must make a definite, eternal decision. Sometimes a sinner finds himself so pressed by the Spirit that he must be saved at once or be lost forever.

God's Spirit will not always strive with man. Sometimes He ceases His warning, His pleading; then one cannot be saved because he will not want to be saved.

I was holding revival services in the open air in east Dallas many years ago. On this one night a number had been saved. As a few workers sat about planning and rejoicing over God's blessings, a man came running down the sidewalk. He turned into the lot where the meetings were being held under the stars. Panting and deeply agitated, he said, "O Brother Rice! I'm so glad you're still here!"

He told how he had heard my sermon that evening, was

deeply moved but had resisted God's call. He said that after the service he went home. Every step the Spirit struggled with him and warned him. He said something like this:

"As I walked those six blocks, something told me that tonight was my chance to be saved, that I would run an awful risk if I went home without Christ. But I walked on. When I turned into my own yard, the Holy Spirit seemed to say, 'This is your last call. If you don't get saved tonight, you will never get saved. It is now or never.'

"When I stepped upon the porch, the Holy Spirit seemed to say, 'If you walk into that house unsaved, I will never again speak to you about this matter. I will never again convict you, I will never again warn you.' When I had a hand on the doorknob, God seemed to cry out to me, 'This is your last warning! It is now or never!'

"I turned and ran the six blocks back to this place to see you. Oh, I must get saved tonight!"

He gave himself to Christ and went home with peace and forgiveness. I do not doubt that God really spoke to him as he said, for God "will not always strive with man!"

In a blessed union campaign in the Binghamton Theater in Binghamton, New York, one night I saw out in the audience a man deeply concerned. As friends talked with him about his soul, sweat broke out on his forehead. He forcibly grasped the seat before him as I pleaded from the platform. The congregation sang so earnestly! The Spirit of God struggled with him.

Suddenly this man fell over in a faint. Friends carried him out into the zero weather where he was revived. One man said to him, "Stay here with your friend while I get my car to take you home." But the one who had fainted said, "No! Wait! I must go back into the theater; I must get this matter settled tonight!" When they remonstrated with him that he was sick, he replied, "But this is my last chance! I know it! God has told me that if I do not settle my salvation tonight, I will never be saved."

He came back in. The service had already dismissed, but he came to the wings on the stage, called for me, and said he knew he must get saved that night. Thank God—he was!

Are you burdened about your soul? Then you have not committed the unpardonable sin. Revelation 22:17 proves that *whosoever will* may take the water of life. If you had committed the unpardonable sin, your heart would be like ice. You would have no concern over your soul. You would not be reading this sermon.

I have had conferences with and letters from many who feared they had committed the unpardonable sin. I am sure none of them had. First, a Christian never commits an unpardonable sin since his sins—past and future—are already pardoned. Second, if a lost sinner is burdened about his soul and convicted, then the Spirit has not departed from him. God's Holy Spirit is still striving. That is what makes him want to be saved, what makes him concerned. That is why he is convicted.

O friend, if the Spirit speaks to your heart, I beg you—be saved! God's Spirit will not always strive with you!

Sudden Destruction May Come When God's Spirit Withdraws

The Holy Spirit warns the sinner, pleads with the sinner, strives again and again with the Christ-rejecting sinner. Then at long last God's patience wears out. That may mean that a sinner commits the unpardonable sin, as we have said, in such an attitude toward the wooing of the Spirit that he can never be convicted, never want to repent, never will be saved. No one can be saved without the working of the Spirit on his heart.

But often God's wrath is expressed in sudden destruction. Often He sends terrible and sudden death when His patience wears out. His Holy Spirit will no longer be insulted or ignored.

This is what happened to the hosts who went on in their wild and sinful way before the Flood. When God's patience wore out after long, long years of pleading, the Spirit ceased to strive; then came the Flood. A brief calculation based on Genesis 5 will show that in the seventeen hundred years or so from the birth of Seth until the Flood, with men and women normally living hundreds of years to bear children, the earth was filled with its millions. And these millions who died in the Flood died as an eternal warning of the wrath of God. God's patience wore out. And when God's Spirit ceased to strive, then came sudden destruction.

This is the solemn warning of Proverbs 29:1—"He, that being often reproved hardeneth his neck, shall suddenly be destroyed, and that without remedy."

We know that death often comes to God's own because of their sins. We read in 1 Corinthians 11:29, "For he that eateth and drinketh unworthily, eateth and drinketh damnation to himself, not discerning the Lord's body." Damnation here must mean sickness and death, for the next verse says, "For this cause many are weak and sickly among you, and many sleep." Some at Corinth went to the Lord's Table while drunk or ate of the Lord's Supper unworthily, for many were weak and sickly, and some even died. "Sleep" is a New Testament term for one who has gone to be with the Lord.

In one church a number of members, for selfish and worldly reason, were rejoined in a conspiracy against the pastor, a godly soul-winner. He laid the matter before the Lord and left it there.

Of that small circle, three men soon died who were apparently in splendid health—two after very brief sicknesses and one suddenly with heart failure. I feel reasonably sure they were saved, but as disobedient children they hardened their hearts when reproved often; so physically they were suddenly destroyed.

You preachers, assailed and slandered by self-willed, worldly-minded, rule-or-ruin church members and officers, take the matter directly to the Lord. Be faithful to rebuke sin in the Spirit of Christ; then expect God to bring judgment when necessary.

But those under discussion in Genesis 6:3 are lost people. When God said, "My Spirit shall not always strive with man," He had in mind the wrestling of the Spirit with the lost, trying to bring them to repentance and salvation. Principally of the unsaved did God say in Proverbs 29:1, "He, that being often reproved hardeneth his neck, shall suddenly be destroyed, and that without remedy."

How often have I seen the wicked, after great conviction, after rejecting earnest pleading, be suddenly struck down!

As a teenager in west Texas, on a Saturday night during revival services I felt led to speak to a friend. I said, "Roy, this is the time to go. God is speaking to your heart. And if you will come to Christ, friends of yours will probably be saved, too. Roy, won't you come?"

Roy, older than I, said, "I will not go tonight; I am not ready."

After further pleading proved useless, I left him.

One week went by. The next Saturday afternoon he came to town driving a colt tied to a breaking cart. Someone, in the rough cowboy idea of fun, sailed his Stetson hat at the young horse, causing him to bolt. My friend was jerked from the cart. He got up, seemingly unhurt, dusted himself, and laughed with the rest.

Someone caught the wild colt, and soon the young man was driving home.

His father and brothers later found him unconscious on a country road. The fall from the cart had injured him, causing a blood clot to form on the brain. The next day he died.

How little did either of us suspect that less than a week from the time I had urged him to trust Christ he would be dead! His Christian father had often spoken to his son about this matter and had asked prayer for him many a time. Others, too, had talked with him.

"He, that being often reproved hardeneth his neck, shall suddenly be destroyed." God's Spirit does not always continue to strive! When God's patience wears out, sometimes there is sudden destruction.

How many are now dead and in hell who have heard me preach the gospel to them! In a number of cases unsaved men, after rejecting the gospel and resisting the Holy Spirit, have died suddenly within a few hours after hearing my message.

In Waxahachie, Texas, a garage man heard me one evening, was deeply concerned but turned down the Savior. The next evening he was suddenly killed in an accident.

In the same city and the following night a man who two nights before had attended the services, who had heard the gospel in a stern message of warning, was shot through the heart by an unknown assailant. His wife and daughters had heard me predict that I feared someone would go to meet God suddenly within twenty-four hours. I was asked to conduct his funeral.

I have often related the incident of a young man who heard me preach one night in Roosevelt, Oklahoma. He was warned by his mother at lunch the next day, and at about 1:40 P.M. he was killed by a train.

I have told how a young Indian at Kaw, Oklahoma, was invited to hear me preach but laughed the matter off, and that night while lying drunk on the railroad track was cut in two by a train.

"My Spirit shall not always strive with man." And the stern warning is, "He, that being often reproved hardeneth his neck, shall suddenly be destroyed, and that without remedy."

If you do not like this kind of preaching, then you are against the Bible. No doubt those in Noah's day didn't like it either. They may have thought., "We don't want to hear deathbed tales from the pulpit." No doubt they said, "You can't scare us with that kind of preaching. Why don't you preach on the love of God?" Well, the love of God needs to be preached, but so does the wrath of God. God's patience, His long-suffering, His infinite mercy ought to be proclaimed; then we ought to proclaim that God's Spirit will not always strive with man, that the man who being often reproved and hardens his heart shall suddenly be destroyed with irremediable destruction!

That famous evangelist of a past generation, Sam Jones, told of case after case where men who had often been warned of their sin and urged to repent had died suddenly. Other great men whom God has used have related incident after incident where men died suddenly who rejected Christ. Yes, God's patience does wear out!

O sinner, turn and be saved while you can! Run to the Savior's open arms of mercy! Before the Holy Spirit leaves you, before God's Spirit ceases to strive, before His patience wears out, turn and be saved! For those who repent there is mercy and pardon and life everlasting.

God's Spirit may not call tomorrow, so today heed the warning of Isaiah 55:6, 7:

"Seek ye the Lord while he may be found, call ye upon him while he is near: Let the wicked forsake his way, and the unrighteous man his thoughts; and let him return unto the Lord, and he will have mercy upon him; and to our God, for he will abundantly pardon."

God's Spirit will not always strive with men. But He is striving with you today. You are conscious of your guilt. You know you must one day meet God, prepared or not. Will you take advantage of your opportunity, repent of your sins, trust Christ to save you today before God's patience wears out?

Robert G. Lee
1886-1978

As pastor and author, Lee was also one of the greatest preachers in the Southern Baptist Convention. He attended Furman University after working on the Panama Canal construction project to earn school money.

He was awarded eleven honorary doctorates, prepared fifty books of sermons, served as president of the Tennessee Baptist Convention four times, and served as president of the Southern Baptist Convention for three consecutive terms. In addition to other pastorates, he served thirty-three years as pastor of Bellevue Baptist Church in Memphis, Tennessee, where the membership grew from 1,739 to 9,469. Additions totaled 24,071, and baptisms numbered 7,649. He authored fifty-six books and wrote many articles and pamphlets.

This famous sermon, "Payday Someday," was delivered 1,275 times. It demonstrates his gift of eloquent, descriptive, and forceful expression. As in all his sermons, his thoughts and words are centered on the terror and beauty of the majesty of God—always calling sinners to repentance and salvation.

"Payday Someday" was also filmed and made into a sacred opera. The technicolored film has been shown in many churches throughout the United States as well as other countries.

Payday
Someday

*Arise, go down to meet Ahab king of Israel, which is in
Samaria: behold, he is in the vineyard of Naboth, whither he
is gone down to possess it. And thou shalt speak unto him,
saying, Thus saith the Lord, Hast thou killed, and also taken
possession? And thou shalt speak unto him, saying, Thus
saith the Lord, In the place where dogs licked the blood of
Naboth shall dogs lick thy blood, even thine. . . . And of
Jezebel also spake the Lord, saying, The dogs shall eat Jezebel
by the wall of Jezreel. (1 Kings 21: 18, 19, 23)*

I introduce to you Naboth. Naboth was a devout Israelite who
lived in the town of Jezreel. Naboth was a good man. He
abhorred that which is evil. He clave to that which is good.
He would not dilute the stringency of his personal piety for any
profit in money. He would not change his heavenly principles for
loose expediences. And this good man who loved God, his family,
and his nation had a little vineyard which was close by the summer palace of Ahab, the king—a palace unique in its splendor as
the first palace inlaid with ivory. This little vineyard had come to
Naboth as a cherished inheritance from his forefathers—and all
of it was dear to his heart.

I introduce to you Ahab, the vile human toad who squatted
upon the throne of his nation—the worst of Israel's kings. King
Ahab had command of a nation's wealth and a nation's army, but
he had no command of his lusts and appetites. Ahab wore rich
robes, but he had a sinning and wicked and troubled heart be-
neath them. He ate the finest food the world could supply—and
this food was served to him in dishes splendid by servants obedi-
ent to his every beck and nod—but he had a starved soul. He
lived in palaces sumptuous within and without; yet he tormented

himself for one bit of land more. Ahab was a king with a throne and a crown and a scepter; yet he lived nearly all of his life under the thumb of a wicked woman—a tool in her hands. Ahab pilloried himself in the contempt of all God-fearing men as a mean and selfish rascal who was the curse of his country. The Bible introduces him to us in words more appropriate than these when it says:

> But there was none like unto Ahab, which did sell himself
> to work wickedness in the sight of the Lord, whom Jezebel
> his wife stirred up. And he did very abominably in
> following idols, according to all things as did the Amorites,
> whom the Lord cast out before the children of Israel. . . .
> And Ahab made a grove; and Ahab did more to provoke
> the Lord God of Israel to anger than all the kings of Israel
> that were before him. (1 Kings 21: 25, 26; 16:33)

I introduce to you Jezebel, daughter of Ethbaal, King of Tyre (1 Kings 16:31), and wife of Ahab, the King of Israel—a king's daughter and a king's wife, the evil genius at once of her dynasty and of her country. Infinitely more daring and reckless was she in her wickedness than was her wicked husband. Masterful, indomitable, implacable, a devout worshiper of Baal, she hated anyone and everyone who spoke against or refused to worship her pagan god. As blunt in her wickedness and as brazen in her lewdness was she as Cleopatra, fair sorceress of the Nile. She had all the subtle and successful scheming of Lady Macbeth, all the adulterous desire and treachery of Potiphar's wife (Genesis 39:7-20), all the boldness of Mary Queen of Scots, all the cruelty and whimsical imperiousness of Catherine of Russia, all the devilish infamy of a Madame Pompadour, and, doubtless, all the fascination of personality of a Josephine of France.

Most of that which is bad in all evil women found expression through this painted viper of Israel. She had that rich endowment of nature which a good woman ought always to dedicate to the service of her day and generation. But—alas!—this idolatrous daughter of an idolatrous king of an idolatrous people engaging with her maidens in worship unto Ashtoreth—the personification of the most forbidding obscenity, uncleanness, and sensuality—the evil genius who wrought wreck, brought blight and devised death. She was the beautiful and malicious adder coiled upon the throne of the nation.

I introduce to you Elijah the Tishbite, prophet of God at a time when by tens of thousands the people had forsaken God's covenants, thrown down God's altars, slain God's prophets with the sword (1 Kings 19:10). The prophet, knowing much of the glorious past of the now apostate nation, must have been filled with horror when he learned of the rank heathenism, fierce cruelties, and reeking licentiousness of Ahab's idolatrous capital. Holy anger burned within him like an unquenchable Vesuvius. He wore the roughest kind of clothes, but he had underneath these clothes a righteous and courageous heart. He ate bird's food and widow's fare, but he was a great physical and spiritual athlete. He was God's tall cedar that wrestled with the paganistic cyclones of his day without bending or breaking. He was God's granite wall that stood up and out against the rising tides of the apostasy of his day. Though much alone, he was sometimes attended by the invisible hosts of God. He grieved only when God's cause seemed tottering. He passed from earth without dying—into celestial glory. Everywhere courage is admired and manhood honored and service appreciated, he is honored as one of earth's greatest heroes and one of heaven's greatest saints. He was a seer who saw clearly. He was a great heart who felt deeply. He was a hero who dared valiantly.

And now with the introduction of these four characters— Naboth, the devout Jezreelite—Ahab, the vile human toad who squatted befoulingly on the throne of the nation—Jezebel, the beautiful adder beside the toad—and Elijah, the prophet of the living God, I bring you the tragedy of "Payday Someday."

And the first scene in the tragedy of "Payday Someday" is:

The Real Estate Request

"Give me thy vineyard"

And it came to pass after these things, that Naboth the Jezreelite had a vineyard, which was in Jezreel, hard by the palace of Ahab king of Samaria. And Ahab spake unto Naboth, saying, Give me thy vineyard, that I may have it for a garden of herbs, because it is near unto my house: and I will give thee for it a better vineyard than it, or, if it seem good to thee, I will give thee the worth of it in money. (1 Kings 21:1, 2)

Thus far Ahab was quite within his rights. No intention had he of cheating Naboth out of his vineyard or of killing him to get it. Honestly did he offer to give him its worth in money. Honestly did he offer him a better vineyard for it. Perfectly fair and square was Ahab in this request and, under circumstances ordinary, one would have expected Naboth to put away any mere sentimental attachment which he had for his ancestral inheritance in order that he might please the king of his nation—especially when the king's aim was not to defraud or rob him.

Ahab had not, however, counted upon the reluctance of all Jews to part with their inheritance of land. By peculiar tenure every Israelite held his land, and to all land-holding transactions there was another party, even God, "who made the heavens and the earth." Throughout Judah and Israel, Jehovah was the real owner of the soil; and every tribe received its territory and every family its inheritance by lot from Him, with the added condition that the land should not be sold forever.

> The land shall not be sold for ever: for the land is mine; for ye are strangers and sojourners with Me. . . . So shall not the inheritance of the children of Israel remove from tribe to tribe: for every one of the children of Israel shall keep himself to the inheritance of the tribe of his fathers . . . but every one of the tribes of the children of Israel shall keep himself to his own inheritance. (Leviticus 25:23; Numbers 36:7, 9)

Thus we see that the permanent sale of the paternal inheritance was forbidden by law. Ahab forgot—if he had ever really known it—that for Naboth to sell for money or to swap for a better vineyard his little vineyard would seem to that good man like a denial of his allegiance to the true religion when jubileee restoration was neglected in such idolatrous times.

So, though he was Ahab's nearest neighbor, Naboth, with religious scruples blended with the pride of ancestry, stood firmly on his rights—and, with an expression of horror on his face and with tones of terror in his words, refused to sell or swap his vineyard to the king. Feeling that he must prefer the duty he owed to God to any danger that might arise from man, he made firm refusal. With much fear of God and little fear of man he said: "The Lord forbid it me, that I should give the inheritance of my fathers unto thee" (1 Kings 21:3).

True to the religious teachings of his father, with loyalty to the covenant God of Israel, he believed that he held the land in fee simple from God. His father and grandfather, and doubtless grandfather's father, had owned the land before him. All the memories of childhood were tangled in its grapevines. His father's hands, folded now in the dust of death, had used the pruning blade among the branches, and because of this every branch and vine was dear. His mother's hands, now doubtless wrapped in a dust-stained shroud, had gathered purple clusters from these bunch-laden boughs, and for this reason he loved every spot in his vineyard and every branch on his vines. The ties of sentiment, of religion, and of family pride bound and endeared him to the place. So his refusal to sell was quick, firm, final, and courteous. Then, too, doubtless working or resting or strolling as he often did in his vineyard hard by the king's castle, Naboth had had glimpses of strange and alien sights in the palace. He had seen with his own eyes what orgies idolatry led to when the queen was at home in her palace in Jezreel; and Naboth, deeply pious, felt smirched and hurt at the very request. He felt that his little plot of ground, so rich in prayer and fellowship, so sanctified with sweet and holy memories, would be tainted and befouled and cursed forever if it came into the hands of Jezebel. So with "the courage of a bird that dares the wild sea," he took his stand against the king's proposal.

And that brings us to the second scene in this tragedy. It is:

The Pouting Potentate

"He came into his house heavy and displeased."

Naboth's quick, firm, courteous, final refusal took all the spokes from the wheels of Ahab's desires and plans. Naboth's refusal was a barrier that turned aside the stream of Ahab's desire and changed it into a foiled and foaming whirlpool of sullen sulks.

And Ahab came into his house heavy and displeased because of the word which Naboth the Jezreelite had spoken to him: for he had said, I will not give thee the inheritance of my fathers. And he laid him down upon his bed, and turned away his face, and would eat no bread. (1 Kings 21:4)

101

What a ridiculous picture! A king acting like a spoiled and sullen child—impotent in disappointment and ugly in petty rage! A king whose victories over the Syrians have rung through many lands— a conquerer, a slave to himself—whining like a sick hound! A king, rejecting all converse with others, pouting like a spoiled and petulant child who has been denied one trinket in the midst of one thousand playthings! A king, in a chamber "ceiled with cedar, and painted with vermilion" (Jeremiah 22:14), prostituting genius to theatrical trumpery.

Ahab went into his ivory house, while the sun was shining and the matters of the daytime were all astir, and went to bed and "turned his face to the wall"—his lips swollen with his mulish moping, his eyes burning with cheap anger-fire, his wicked heart stubborn in perverse rebellion against the commandments of God. Servants brought him his meal, plenteously prepared on platters beautiful, but he "would eat no bread." Doubtless, musicians came to play skillfully on stringed instruments, but he drove them all away with imperious gestures and impatient growlings. He turned from his victuals as one turns from garbage and refuse. The conqueror of the Syrians is a low slave to dirt-cheap trivialities. His spirit, now devilishly sullen, is in bondage.

What an ancient picture we have of great powers dedicated to mean, ugly, petty things. Think of it! In the middle of the day, the commander-in-chief of an army seized by Sergeant Sensitive. General Ahab made prisoner by Private Pouts! The leader of an army laid low by Corporal Mopishness! A monarch moaning and blubbering and growlingly refusing to eat because a man, a good man, because of the commandments of God and because of religious principles, would not sell or swap a little vineyard which was his by inheritance from his forefathers. Ahab had lost nothing—had gained nothing. No one had injured him. No one had made attempt on his life. Yet he, a king with a great army and a fat treasury, was acting like a blubbering baby. Cannon ability was expressing itself in popgun achievement. A massive giant sprawling on the bed like a dwarf punily peevish! A whale wallowing and spouting angrily about because he is denied minnow food! A bear growling sulkily because he cannot lick a spoon in which is a bit of honey! An eagle shrieking and beating his wings in the dust of his own displeasure like a quarreling sparrow fussily fighting with other sparrows for the crumbs in the dust of a village street!

A lion sulkily roaring because he was not granted the cheese in a mousetrap! A battleship cruising for a beetle!

What an ancient picture of giant powers and talents prostituted to base and purposeless ends and withheld from the service of God! What an ancient spectacle! And how modern and up-to-date, in this respect, was Ahab, King of Israel. What a likeness to him in conduct today are many talented men and women. I know men and women—you know men and women—with diamond and ruby abilities who are worth no more to God through the churches than a punctured Japanese nickel in a Chinese bazaar! So many there are who, like Ahab, withhold their talents from God—using them in the service of the Devil. People there are, not a few, who have pipe-organ abilities and make no more music for the causes of Christ than a wheezy saxophone in an idiot's hands. People there are, many of them, who have incandescent light powers who make no more light for God than a smoky barn lantern, with smoke-blackened globe, on a stormy night. People there are—I know them and you know them—with locomotive powers doing pushcart work for God. People there are—and how sad 'tis true—who have steam-shovel abilities who are doing teaspoon work for God. Yes! Now look at this overfed bull bellowing for a little spot of grass outside his own vast pasture lands—and, if you are withholding talents and powers from the service of God, receive the rebuke of the tragic and ludicrous picture.

And now, consider the third scene in this tragedy of "Payday Someday." It is:

The Wicked Wife

"And Jezebel his wife . . ."

When Ahab would "eat no bread," the servants went and told Jezebel. What she said to them, we do not know. Something of what she said to Ahab we do know. Puzzled and provoked at the news that her husband would not eat—that he had gone to bed when it was not bedtime—Jezebel went to investigate. She found him in bed with his face turned to the wall, his lips swollen with mulish moping, he eyes burning with cheap anger-fire, his heart stubborn in wicked rebellion. He was groaningly mournful and peevishly petulant—having, up to the moment when she stood by his bedside, refused to eat or cheer up in the least.

Looking at him then, she doubtless, as is the custom with women until this day, put her hand on his forehead to see if he had fever. He had fever—without doubt! He was set on fire of hell, even as is a wicked tongue (James 3:6). Then, in a voice of "sweet" solicitation, she sought the reason of his anger. She asked, to put it in the semislang language of our day: "What's the matter with you, Big Boy?" But, in the words of the Bible: "Why is thy spirit so sad, that thou eatest no bread?" (1 Kings 21:5). Then, with his mouth full of grouches, with his heart stubborn in rebellion against the commandment of God, he told her, his every word full of mopish petulance.

> Because I spake unto Naboth the Jezreelite, and said unto him, Give me thy vineyard for money; or else, if it please thee, I will give thee another vineyard for it: and he answered, I will not give thee my vineyard. (1 Kings 21:6)

Every word he said stung like a whip upon a naked back this wickedly unscrupulous woman who had never had any regard for the welfare of anyone who did not worship her god, Baal—who never had any conscientious regard for the rights of others, or for others who did not yield to her whimsical imperiousness.

Hear her derisive laugh as it rings out in the palace like the shrill cackle of a wild fowl that has returned to its nest and has found a serpent therein! With her tongue, sharp as a razor, she prods Ahab as an ox driver prods with sharp goad the ox which does not want to press his neck into the yoke, or as one whips with a rawhide a stubborn mule. With profuse and harsh laughter this old gay and gaudy guinea of Satan derided this king of hers for a cowardly buffoon and sordid jester: What hornetlike sting in her sarcasm! What wolf-mouth fierceness in her every reproach! What tiger-fang cruelty in her expressed displeasure! What fury in the shrieking of her rebuke! What bitterness in the teasing taunts she hurled at him for his scrupulous timidity! Her bosom with anger was heaving! Her eyes were flashing with rage under the surge of hot anger that swept over her.

"Are you not the king of this country?" she chides bitingly, her tongue sharp like a butcher's blade. "Can you not command and have it done?" she scolds as a common village hag who has more noise than wisdom in her words. "Can you not seize and keep?" she cries with reproach. "I thought you told me you were king in these parts! And here you are crying like a baby and will not eat anything because you do not have courage to take a bit of land. You! Ha! Ha! Ha! Ha! You, the King of Israel, allow yourself to be disobeyed and defied by a common clodhopper from the country. You are more courteous and considerate of him than you are of your queen! Shame on you! But you leave it to me! I will get the vineyard for you, and all that I require is that you ask no questions. Leave it to me, Ahab!"

> And Jezebel his wife said unto him, Dost thou now govern the kingdom of Israel? arise, and eat bread, and let thine heart be merry: I will give thee the vineyard of Naboth the Jezreelite. (1 Kings 21:7)

Ahab knew Jezebel well enough to know that she would do her best, or her worst, to keep her wicked promise. So, as a turtle that has been sluggish in the cold winter's mud begins to move when the spring sunshine warms the mud, Ahab crawled out of the slime of his sulks—somewhat as a snake arouses and uncoils from winter sleep. Then Jezebel doubtless tickled him under the chin with her bejeweled fingers or kissed him peckingly on the cheek with her lips screwed in a tight knot, and said: "There now! Smile! And eat something. I will get thee the vineyard of Naboth the Jezreelite!"

Now, let us ask, who can so inspire a man to noble purposes as a noble woman? And who can so thoroughly degrade a man as a wife of unworthy tendencies? Back of the statement, "And Ahab the son of Omri did evil in the sight of the Lord above all that were before him" (1 Kings 16:30), and back of what Elijah spoke, "Thou hast sold thyself to work evil in the sight of the Lord" (1 Kings 21:20), is the statement explaining both the other statements: "Whom Jezebel his wife stirred up." She was the polluted reservoir from which the streams of his own iniquity found mighty increase. She was the poisonous pocket from which his cruel fangs fed. She was the sulphurous pit wherein the fires of his own iniquity found fuel for intenser burning. She was the Devil's grindstone which furnished sharpening for his weapons of wickedness. . . .

Jezebel stirred Ahab up to more and mightier wickedness

than his own wicked mind could conceive or his own wicked hand could execute.

Let us come to the next terrible scene in this tragedy of sin. The next scene is:

A Message Meaning Murder

"She wrote letters."

Jezebel wrote letters to the elders of Jezreel. And in these letters she made definite and subtle declaration that some terrible sin had been committed in their city, for which it was needful that a fast should be proclaimed in order to avert the wrath of heaven.

> So she wrote letters in Ahab's name, and sealed them with his seal, and sent the letters unto the elders and to the nobles that were in his city, dwelling with Naboth. And she wrote in the letters, saying, Proclaim a fast, and set Naboth on high among the people: and set two men, sons of Belial, before him, to bear witness against him, saying, Thou didst blaspheme God and the king. And then carry him out, and stone him, that he may die. (1 Kings 21:8-10)

This letter, with cynical disregard of decency, was a hideous mockery in the name of religion. Once get the recusant citizen accused of blasphemy, and, by a divine law, the property of the blasphemer and rebel went to the crown. "Justice! How many traitors to sacred truth have dragged the innocent to destruction!"

Surely black ink never wrote a fouler plot or death scheme on white paper since writing was known among men. Every drop had in it the adder's poison. Every syllable of every word of every line of every sentence was full of hate toward him who had done only good continually. Every letter of every syllable was but the thread which, united with other threads, made the hangman's noose for him who had not changed his righteous principles for the whim of a king. The whole letter was a diabolical death-warrant.

The letters being written must be sealed; and the sealing was done, as all these matters of letter writing and sealing were done, by rubbing ink on the seal, moistening the paper, and pressing the seal thereon. And when Jezebel had finished with her iniquitous pen, she asked Ahab for his signet ring; with that ring she affixed the royal seal. She sealed the letters with Ahab's ring (1 Kings 21:8).

When Ahab gave it to her he knew it meant crime of some sort, but he asked no questions. Moreover, Jezebel's deeds showed that when she went down to market, as it were, she would have in her basket a nice vineyard for her husband when she returned. She said to herself: "This man Naboth has refused my honorable lord on religious grounds, and by all the gods of Baal, I will get him yet on these very same grounds." She understood perfectly the passion of a devout Jew for a public fast; and she knew that nothing would keep the Jews away. Every Jew and every member of his household would be there.

"Proclaim a fast!" Fasting has ever been a sign of humiliation before God, of humbling oneself in the dust before the "high and lofty One that inhabiteth eternity." The idea in calling for a fast was clearly to declare that the community was under the anger of God on account of a grave crime committed by one of its members, which crime is to be exposed and punished. Then, too, the fast involved a cessation of work, a holiday, so that the citizens would have time to attend the public gathering.

"Set Naboth on high!" "On high" meant before the bar of justice, not in the seat of honor. "On high" meant in the seat of the accused, and not in the seat to be desired. "On high" meant that Naboth was put where every eye could watch him closely and keenly observe his bearing under the accusation. "And set two men, base fellows, before him." How illegal she was in bringing about his death in a legal way! For the law required two witnesses in all cases where the punishment was death. "At the mouth of two witnesses, or three witnesses, shall he . . . be put to death" (Deuteronomy 17:6). The witnesses required by Jezebel were men of no character, men who would take bribes and swear to any lie for gain.

And let them "bear witness against him"! In other words, put him out of the way by judicial murder, not by private assassination. "And then carry him out, and stone him, that he may die." A criminal was not to be executed within a city, as that would defile it! Thus Christ was crucified outside the walls of Jerusalem! We see that Jezebel took it for granted that Naboth would be condemned.

And so one day, while Naboth worked in his vineyard, the

letters came down to Jezreel. And one evening, while Naboth talked at the cottage door with his sons or neighbors, the message meaning murder was known to the elders of the city. And that night, while he slept with the wife of his bosom, the hounds of death let loose from the kennels of hell by the jewel-adorned fingers of a king's daughter and a king's wife were close on his heels. The message meaning murder was known to many but not to him, until they came and told him that a fast had been proclaimed—proclaimed because God had been offended at some crime and His wrath must be appeased and the threatening anger turned away, and he himself, all unconscious of any offense toward God or the king, was to be set in the place of the accused, even "on high among the people," to be tried as a conspicuous criminal.

Consider now:

The Fatal Fast

"They proclaimed a fast."

And what concern they must have created in the household of Naboth, when they knew that Naboth was to be "set on high," even in the "seat of the accused," even before the bar of "justice," because of a ferocious message calling religion in to attest a lie. And what excitement there was in the city when, with fawning readiness to carry out her vile commands, the elders and nobles "fastened the minds" of the people upon the fast—proclaimed as if some great calamity were overhanging the city for their sins like a black cloud portending a storm, and proclaimed as if something must be done at once to avert the doom. Curious throngs hurried to the fast to see him who had been accused of the crime which made necessary the appeasing of the threatening wrath of an angered God.

Yes, the rulers of Jezreel, "either in dread of offending one whose revenge they knew was terrible, or eager to do a service to one to whom in temporal matters they were so largely indebted, or moved with envy against their own iniquity, carried out her instructions to the letter." They were ready and efficient tools in her hands. No doubt she had tested their character as her "butcher boys" in the slaughter of the prophets of the Lord (1 Kings 18:4, 13).

And they did! "And there came in two men, children of
Belial, and sat down before him" (1 Kings 21:13). Satan's hawks
ready to bring death to God's harmless sparrow! Satan's eagles
ready to bury their cruel talons in God's innocent dove! Satan's
bloody wolves ready to kill God's lamb! Satan's boars ready with
keen tusks to rip God's stag to shreds! Reckless and depraved
professional perjurers they were! "And the men of Belial wit-
nessed against him, even against Naboth, in the presence of the
people, saying Naboth did blaspheme God and the king" (1 Kings
21:13).

Then strong hands jerked Naboth out of the seat of the
accused. Doubtless muttering curses the while, they dragged him
out from among the throngs of people, while children screamed
and cried, while women shrieked in terror, while men moved in
confusion and murmured in consternation. They dragged him
roughly to a place outside the walls of the city, and with stones
they beat his body to the ground. Naboth fell to the ground as a
lily by hailstones beaten to earth, as a stately cedar uprooted by
furious storm. His head by stones is crushed, as eggs crushed by
the heel of a giant. His legs are splintered. His arms are broken.
His ribs are crushed. Bones stick out from the mass of human
flesh as fingers of ivory from pots of red paint. Brains, emptied
from his skull, are scattered about. Blood splatters like crimson
rain. Naboth's eyes roll in sockets of blood. His tongue between
broken jaws becomes still. His mauled body becomes—at last—
still. His last gasp is a sigh. Naboth is dead—dead for cursing God
and the king as many were led to believe!

And we learn from 2 Kings 9:26 that by the savage law of
those days his innocent sons were involved in his overthrow.
They, too, that they might not claim the inheritance, were slain.
And Naboth's property, left without heirs, reverted to the crown.

Thus it came to pass that in an orderly fashion, in the name
of religion and in the name of the king, Naboth really fell, not by
the king's hand, but by the condemnation of his fellow citizens.
Yes, the old-fashioned conservatism of Naboth was, in the judgment of many, sorely out of place in that "progressive" state of
society. No doubt Naboth's righteous austerity had made him
extremely unpopular in many ways in "progressive Jezreel." And
since Jezebel carried out her purpose in a perfectly legal and
orderly way and in a "wonderfully" democratic manner, we see a
fine picture of autocracy working by democratic methods. And

when these "loyally patriotic citizens" of Jezreel had left the bodies of Naboth and his sons to be devoured by the wild dogs which prowled after nightfall in and around the city, they sent and told Queen Jezebel that her orders had been bloodily and completely obeyed! "Then they sent to Jezebel, saying, Naboth is stoned, and is dead" (1 Kings 21:14).

I do not know where Jezebel was when she received the news of Naboth's death. Maybe she was out on the lawn watching the fountains splash. Maybe she was in the sun parlor, or somewhere listening to the musicians thrum on their instruments. But if I judge this painted human viper by her nature, I say she received the tragic news with devilish delight, with jubilant merriment.

What was it to her that yonder, over twenty miles away, sat a little woman who the night before had her husband but who now washed his crushed and ghastly face with her tears? What did it matter to her that in Jezreel only yesterday her sons ran to her at her call but today were mangled in death? What did it matter to her that outside the city walls the dogs licked the blood of a godly husband? What mattered it to her that Jehovah God had been defied, His commandments broken, His altars splattered with pagan mud, His holy name profaned? What mattered it to her that the worship of God had been dishonored? What did she care if a wife, tragically widowed by murder, walked life's way in loneliness? What did she care that there was lamentation and grief and great mourning, "Rachel weeping for her children because they were not"? What did she care if justice had been outraged just so she had gotten the little plot of land close by their palace, within which was evil girt with diadem? Nothing! Did pang grip her heart because innocent blood had been shed? Just as well ask if the ravenous lion mourns over the lamb it devours.

Trippingly, as a gay dancer, she hurried to where Ahab sat. With profuse caresses and words glib with joy she told him the "good" news. She had about her the trimphant manner of one who has accomplished successfully what others had not dared attempt. Her "tryout" in getting the vineyard was a decided "triumph." She had "pulled the stunt." She had been "brave" and "wise"—and because of this her husband now could arise and hie him down to the vineyard and call it his own.

In her words and manner there was jubilant elation bordering on the Satanic. "Arise!" she said. "Get thee down and take possession of the vineyard of Naboth! I told thee I would get his vineyard for thee. And I got for nothing what thou wast going to give a better vineyard for!"

> And it came to pass, when Jezebel heard that Naboth was stoned, and was dead, that Jezebel said to Ahab, Arise, take possession of the vineyard of Naboth the Jezreelite, which he refused to give thee for money: for Naboth is not alive, but dead. (1 Kings 21:15)

It was the plot hatched in her own mind and it was her hand, her lily-white hand, her queen's hand, that wrote the letters that made this tragic statement true.

The next scene in this tragedy of "Payday Someday" is:

The Visit to the Vineyard

"Ahab rose up to go down to the vineyard."

How Jezebel must have paraded with pride before Ahab when she went with tidings that the vineyard which he wanted to buy was now his for nothing! How keen must have been the sarcasm of her attitude when she made it known by word and manner that she had succeeded where he failed—and at less cost! How gloatingly victorious were the remarks which she made which kept him warmly reminded that she had kept her "sacred" promise! What a lovely fabric, stained and dyed red with Naboth's blood, she spread before him for his "comfort" from the loom of her evil machinations!

"And it came to pass, when Ahab heard that Naboth was dead, that Ahab rose up to go down to the vineyard of Naboth the Jezreelite, to take possession of it" (1 Kings 21:16). Ahab rose up to go down—from Samaria to Jezreel. He gave orders to his royal wardrobe keeper to get out his king's clothes, because he had a little "business" trip to make to look over some property that had come to him by the shrewdness of his wife in the real estate market!

Yes, Naboth, the good man who "feared the Lord," is dead; and Ahab expresses no condemnation of this awful conspiracy, culminating in such a tragic horror. Though afraid or restrained by his conscience from committing murder himself, he had no scruple in availing himself of the results of such crime when perpetrated by another. He flattered himself that by the splendid genius of his queen in bloody matters, he, though having no part in the crime which did Naboth to death, might, as well as another, "receive the benefit of his dying."

And you will notice just here that not one noble or elder had divulged the terrible secret which had given the semblance of legality to atrocious villainy. And Ahab, rejoicing in the bloody garment woven on the loom of his wife's evil machinations, gave orders to those in charge of livery stables to get ready his royal chariot for an unexpected trip. Jehu and Bidkar, the royal chario-teers, made ready the great horses such as kings had in those days.

Jehu was the speed-breaking driver of his day, known as the one who drove furiously. The gilded chariot is drawn forth. The fiery horses are harnessed and to the king's chariot hitched. The outriders, in gorgeous garments dressed, saddle their horses and make ready to accompany the king in something of military state. Then, amid the clatter of prancing hoofs and the loud breathing of the chariot horses—eager-eyed, alert, strong-muscled, bellows-lunged, stouthearted, and agile of feet—Jehu drives the horses and the chariot up to the palace steps.

Out from the palace doors, with Jezebel walking, almost strut-ting, proudly and gaily at his side, comes Ahab. Down the steps he goes while Jezebel perhaps waves a bejeweled hand to him or speaks a "sweet" good-bye. Bidkar opens the chariot door. Ahab steps in. Then, with the crack of his whip or a sharp command by word of mouth, Jehu sends the great horses on their way—away from the palace steps, away from the palace grounds, away through the gates, away, accompanied by the outriders, away down the road to Jezreel!

Where is God? Where is God? Is He blind that He cannot see? Is He deaf that He cannot hear? Is He dumb that He cannot speak? Is He paralyzed that He cannot move? *Where is God?* Well, wait a minute, and we shall see.

Over there in the palace Jezebel said to Ahab her husband: "Arise! Get thee down and take possession of the vineyard of Naboth." And over in the wilderness way, out where the tall cedars waved against the moon like green plumes against a silver shield, out where the only music of the night was the weird call of whippoorwill and the cough of coyote and the howl of wolf, out there God had an eagle-eyed, hairy, stout-hearted prophet, a great physical and spiritual athlete, Elijah. "And the word of the Lord came to Elijah." And God said to Elijah: "Arise, go down."

Over here, in the palace, Jezebel said to Ahab: "Arise, get thee down!" And out there, near Carmel, God said to Elijah: "Arise!" I am so glad that I live in a universe where, when the Devil has his Ahab to whom he can say, "Arise," God has His Elijah to whom *He* can say, "Arise!"

> And the word of the Lord came to Elijah the Tishbite, saying, Arise, go down to meet Ahab king of Israel, which is in Samaria: behold he is in the vineyard of Naboth, whither he is gone down to possess it. And thou shalt speak unto him, saying, Thus saith the Lord, Hast thou killed, and also taken possession? And thou shalt speak unto him, saying, Thus saith the Lord, In the place where dogs licked the blood of Naboth, shall dogs lick thy blood, even thine. (1 Kings 21:17-19)

As Ahab goes down to Jezreel, the voice of Jehu as he restrains the fiery horses, or the lash of his whip as he urges them on, attracts the attention of the grazing cattle in adjacent pastureland. The sound of clanking hoofs of cantering horses resounds in every glen by the roadway. The gilded chariot catches the light of the sun and reflects it brightly, but he who rides therein is unmindful of the bloodstains on the ground where Naboth died. Dust clouds arise from the chariot's wheels and wild winds blow them across the fields where the plowman or the reaper wonders who goes so swiftly along the highway.

The neighing steeds announce to all that Ahab's royal horses tire not in carrying him down from Samaria to Jezreel. And soon many know that the chariot carried the king who was going down to possess what had reverted to the crown, even the vineyard of Naboth, which Naboth refused to sell to him. Would the "game" be worth the "candle"? Would Ahab learn that sin buys pleasure at the price of peace? We shall see—and that right soon!

And that brings us to the other scene in this tragedy of "Payday Someday." It is:

113

The Alarming Appearance

> *"The word of the Lord came to Elijah."*

The journey of twenty-odd miles from Samaria to Jezreel is over. Jehu brings the horses to a stop outside the gate to the vineyard. The horses stretch their necks trying to get slack on the reins. They have stood well the furious pace at which they have been driven. Around the rim of their harness is the foam of their sweat. On their flanks are perhaps the marks of Jehu's whip. They breathe as though their great lungs were a tireless bellows. The outriders line up in something of military formation. The hands of ready servants open the gate to the vineyard. Bidkar opens the chariot door. And Ahab steps out into Naboth's vineyard.

There, no doubt, he sees in the soft soil Naboth's footprints. Close by, doubtless, the smaller footprints of his wife he sees. Naboth is dead, and the coveted vineyard is now Ahab's through the "gentle scheming" of the queen of his house. Perhaps Ahab, as he walks into the vineyard, sees Naboth's pruning hook among the vines. Or he notices the fine trellis work which Naboth's hands had fastened together for the growing vines. Perhaps in a corner of the vineyard is a seat where Naboth and his sons rested after the day's toil, or a well where sparkling waters refreshed the thirsty or furnished water for the vines in times of drouth.

Ahab walks around his newly-gotten vineyard. The rows of vines glisten in the sunlight. Maybe a breeze moves the leaves on the vines. Ahab admires trellis and cluster. As he walks, he plans how he will have the royal gardener pull up those vines and plant cucumbers, squash, garlic, onions, cabbage, and other vegetables that he may have his "garden of herbs."

And while Ahab strolls among the vines that Naboth tended, what is it that appears? Snarling wild beasts? No. Black clouds full of threatening storm? No, not that. Flaming lightning which dazzles him? No. War chariots of his ancient enemies rumbling along the road? No. An oncoming flood sweeping things before it? No, not a flood. A tornado goring the earth? No. A huge serpent threatening to encircle him and crush his bones in its deadly coils? No, not a serpent. What then? What alarmed Ahab so? Let us follow him and see.

As Ahab goes walking through the rows of vines, he begins to plan how he will have that vineyard arranged by his royal gardener, how flowers will be here and vegetables yonder and herbs there. As he converses with himself, suddenly a shadow falls across his path. Quick as a flash Ahab whirls on his heels, and there before him stands Elijah, prophet of the living God. Elijah's cheeks are swarthy; his eye is keen and piercing; like coals of fire, his eyes burn with righteous indignation in their sockets; his bosom heaves; his head is held high. His only weapon is a staff, his only robe a sheepskin and a leather girdle about his loins.

Like an apparition from the other world, like Banquo's ghost at Macbeth's feast, Elijah, with suddenness terrifying, stands before Ahab. Ahab had not seen Elijah for five years. Ahab thought Elijah had been cowed and silenced by Jezebel, but now the prophet confronts him with his death-warrant from the Lord God Almighty.

To Ahab there is an eternity of agony in the few moments they stand thus, face to face, eye to eye, soul to soul! His voice is hoarse, like the cry of a hunted animal. He trembles like a hunted stag before the mouths of fierce hounds. Suddenly his face goes white. His lips quiver. He had gone to take possession of a vineyard, coveted for a garden of herbs; and there he is face to face with righteousness, face to face with honor, face to face with judgment. The vineyard, with the sun shining upon it now, is as black as if it were part of the midnight which has gathered in judgment. Like Poe's raven "his soul from out that shadow shall be lifted—nevermore."

"And Ahab said to Elijah, Hast thou found me, O mine enemy?" (1 Kings 21:20). And Elijah, without a tremor in his voice, his eyes burning their way into Ahab's guilty soul, answered: "I have found thee: because thou hast sold thyself to work evil in the sight of the Lord." Then, with every word a thunderbolt and every sentence a withering denunciation, Elijah continued:

Hast thou killed, and also taken possession? . . . Thus saith
the Lord, In the place where dogs licked the blood of
Naboth shall dogs lick thy blood, even thine. . . . Behold,
I will bring evil upon thee, and will take away thy
posterity . . . and will make thine house like the house of
Jeroboam the son of Nebat, and like the house of Baasha
the son of Ahijah, for the provocation wherewith thou
hast provoked me to anger and made Israel to sin!
(1 Kings 21:19, 21, 22)

And then, plying other words mercilessly like a terrible scourge to the cringing Ahab, Elijah said:

> And of Jezebel also spake the Lord, saying, The dogs shall eat Jezebel by the wall of Jezreel. Him that dieth of Ahab in the city the dogs shall eat: and him that dieth in the field shall the fowls of the air eat. (1 Kings 21:23, 24)

And with these words making Ahab to cower as one cowers and recoils from a hissing adder, finding Naboth's vineyard to be haunted with ghosts and the clusters thereof to be full of blood, Elijah went his way—as was his custom so suddenly to appear and so quickly to disappear.

Ahab had sold himself for nought, as did Achan for a burial robe and a useless ingot, as did Judas for thirty pieces of silver which so burned his palms and so burned his conscience and so burned his soul that he found relief in the noose at the rope's end. And when Ahab got back in the chariot to go back to Jezebel—the vile toad who squatted upon the throne to be again with the beautiful adder coiled upon the throne—the hoofs of the horses pounding the road pounded into his guilty soul Elijah's words: "Someday the dogs will lick thy blood! Someday the dogs will eat Jezebel—by the ramparts of Jezreel." God had spoken! Would it come to pass?

And now we come to the last scene in this tragedy—"Payday Someday." It is:

Payday Itself

Did God mean what He said? Or was He playing a prank on royalty? Did payday come? "Payday Someday" is written in the constitution of God's universe. The retributive providence of God is a reality as certainly as the laws of gravitation are a reality.

And to Ahab and Jezebel, payday came as certainly as night follows day, because sin carries in itself the seed of its own fatal penalty.

Dr. Meyer says: "According to God's constitution of the world, the wrongdoer will be abundantly punished." The fathers sow the wind, and the children reap the whirlwind. One generation labors to scatter tares, and the next generation reaps tares and retribution immeasurable. To the individual who goes not the direction God points, a terrible payday comes. To the nation which forgets God, payday will come in the awful realization of the truth that the "nations which forget God shall be turned into hell." When nations trample on the principles of the Almighty, the result is that the world is beaten with many stripes. We have seen nations slide into Gehenna—and the smoke of their torment has gone up before our eyes day and night.

To the home that has no room for the Christ, death and grave clothes are certain. "Ichabod" will be written about the church that soft-pedals on unpleasant truth or that stands not unwaveringly for "the faith once delivered"—and it will acknowledge its retribution in that it will become "a drifting sepulchre manned by a frozen crew."

A man can prostitute God's holy name to profane lips if he will, but he is forewarned as to the payday in the words: "The Lord will not hold him guiltless that taketh his Name in vain" (Exodus 20:7).

A man can, if he will, follow the way of some wicked woman; but God leaves him not without warning as to the payday, in the words:

> He goeth after her straightway, as an ox goeth to the
> slaughter, or as a fool to the correction of the stocks; Till a
> dart strike through his liver; as a bird hasteth to the snare,
> and knoweth not that it is for his life. . . . For she hath
> cast down many wounded: yea, many strong men have
> been slain by her. Her house is the way to hell, going
> down to the chambers of death. (Prov. 7:22, 23, 26, 27)

People can drink booze, if they will, and offer the damnable bottle to others, if they will, but the certainty of "Payday Someday" is read in the words: "No drunkard shall inherit the kingdom of God," and in the words: "At the *last* it biteth like a serpent, and stingeth like an adder." The certainty of "Payday Someday" for all who regard not God or man is set forth in the words of an unknown poet:

> You'll pay. The knowledge of your acts will weigh
> Heavier on your mind each day.
> The more you climb, the more you gain,
> The more you'll feel the nagging strain.
> Success will cower at the threat

Of retribution. Fear will fret
Your peace and bleed you for the debt;
Conscience collects from every crook
More than the worth of what he took,
You only thought you got away
But in the night you'll pay and pay.

Churchill expressed the certainty of God's retributive justice
when, speaking of Mussolini, he said:

Mussolini is swept into the maelstrom of his own making.
The flames of war he kindled burn himself. He and his
people are taking the stinging lash of the whip they
applied to Ethiopia and Albania. They pay for Fascist sins
with defeat, despair, death. Mussolini's promise of life like
a lion turns into the existence of a beaten cur!

Years before the statesman Winston Churchill spoke these
words, Ralph Waldo Emerson, in his *Compensation*, wrote:

Crime and punishment grow out of one stem. Punishment
is a fruit that unsuspected ripens within the flower of the
pleasure that concealed it. Cause and effect, means and
ends, seed and fruit, can not be severed, for the effect
already blooms in the cause. The end pre-exists in the
means—the fruit in the seed.

Paul Lawrence Dunbar showed wisdom as great as the wisdom of Churchill and a knowledge of Nature's laws as great as
Emerson's knowledge when he wrote the autobiography of many
individual sinners in these poetic and potent words:

This is the price I pay—
Just for one riotous day—
Years of regret and of grief,
And sorrow without relief.
Suffer it I will, my friend,
Suffer it until the end,
Until the grave shall give relief.
Small was the thing I bought,
Small was the thing at best,
Small was the debt, I thought,
But, O God!—the interest.

All these statements are but verification of Bible truth:

Whoso diggeth a pit shall fall therein: and he that rolleth a stone, it will return upon him. (Proverbs 26:27)

Therefore shall they eat of the fruit of their own way, and be filled with their own devices. For the turning away of the simple shall slay them, and the prosperity of fools shall destroy them. (Proverbs 1:31, 32)

Even as I have seen, they that plow iniquity, and sow wickedness, reap the same. (Job 4:8)

For they have sown the wind, and they shall reap the whirlwind. (Hosea 8:7)

When I was pastor of the First Baptist Church of New Orleans, all that I preached and taught was sent out over the radio. In my "fan mail" I received letters from a young man who called himself "Chief of the Kangaroo Court." Many nasty, critical things he said. Sometimes he wrote a nice line—and a nice line was, in all the vulgar things he wrote, like a gardenia in a garbage can. One day I received a telephone call from a nurse in the Charity Hospital of New Orleans. It was about this fellow who so often dipped his pen in slop, who seldom thrust his pen into nectar. She said: "Pastor, there is a young man down here whose name we do not know, who will not tell us his name. All he will tell us is that he is Chief of the Kangaroo Court. He is going to die. He says that you are the only preacher in New Orleans that he has ever heard—and he has never seen you. He wants to see you. Will you come down?" "Yes," I replied. And I quit what I was doing and hurried down to the hospital.

The young nurse met me at the entrance to the charity ward and took me in. A glance around showed me cots on the north side, cots on the south side, beds on the east side, and beds on the west side—and clusters of cots in the center of the huge ward. In a place by itself, somewhat removed from all other cots and beds, was a bed on which lay a young man about nineteen or twenty years of age—big of frame, though the ravages of disease had brought a slenderness. The nurse, with little ado, introduced me to the young man, saying: "This, sir, is the Chief of the Kangaroo Court."

I found myself looking into two of the wildest, weirdest eyes I have ever seen. As kindly as I could, I spoke, saying "Hello." "Howdy do?" he answered in a voice that was a discourteous and furious snarl—more like the voice of a mad wolf than the voice of a rational man. "Is there something I can do for you?" I asked as kindly as I could speak.

"No. Nothing! Not a thing. Nothin' 'tall!—unless you throw my body to the buzzards when I am dead—if the buzzards will have it!" he said, with half a shout and with a sort of fierce resentment that made me wonder why he had ever sent for me.

Then his voice lost some of the snarl—and he spoke again. "I sent for you, sir, because I want you to tell these young fellows here something for me. I sent for you because I know you go up and down the land and talk to many young people. And I want you to tell 'em, and tell 'em every chance you get, that the Devil pays only in counterfeit money."

Oh, I wish I could tell all men and women and all boys and girls everywhere to believe the truth that Satan always pays in counterfeit money, that all his pearls are paste pearls, that the nectar he offers is poisoned through and through. Oh, that men would learn the truth and be warned by the truth that if they eat the Devil's corn, he will choke them with the cob.

I stayed with this young man nearly two hours. Occasionally he spoke. There was a desperate earnestness in the young man's voice as he looked at me with wild eyes where terror was enthroned. After a while I saw those eyes become as though they were glass as he gazed at the ceiling above. I saw his huge lean chest heave like a bellows. I felt his hand clutch at mine as a drowning man would grab for a rope. I held his hand. I heard the raucous gurgle in his throat. Then he became quiet—like a forest when the cyclone is long gone.

When he died, the little nurse called me to her excitedly. "Come here!" she called.

"What do you want, child?" I asked.

"I want to wash your hands!" She meant she wanted to wash my hands with a disinfectant. Then she added—with something of fright in her words, "It's dangerous to touch him!"

The Devil had paid the young man off in counterfeit money.

But what about Ahab? Did payday come for him? Yes. Consider how. Three years went by. Ahab was still king. And I daresay that during those three years Jezebel had reminded him that they were eating herbs out of Naboth's vineyard. I can hear her say something like this as they sat at the king's table: "Ahab, help yourself to these herbs. I thought Elijah said the dogs were going to lick your blood. I guess his dogs lost their noses and lost the trail."

But I think that during those three years, Ahab never heard a dog bark that he did not jump.

One day Jehoshaphat, king of Judah, visited Ahab. The Bible tells us what took place—what was said, what was done:

> And the king of Israel said unto his servants, Know ye
> that Ramoth in Gilead is ours, and we be still, and take it
> not out of the hand of the king of Syria? And he said
> unto Jehoshaphat, Wilt thou go with me to battle to
> Ramoth-gilead? And Jehoshaphat said to the king of Israel,
> I am as thou art, my people as thy people, my horses as
> thy horses. (1 Kings 22:3, 4)

> So the king of Israel and Jehoshaphat the king of Judah
> went up to Ramoth-gilead. (1 Kings 22:29)

Ahab, after Jehoshaphat had promised to go with him, in his heart was afraid, and had sad forebodings, dreadful premonitions, horrible fears. Remembering the withering words of Elijah three years before, he disguised himself—put armor on his body and covered this armor with ordinary citizen's clothes.

> And the king of Israel said unto Jehoshaphat, I will
> disguise myself, and enter into the battle; but put thou on
> thy robes. And the king of Israel disguised himself, and
> went into the battle. (1 Kings 22:30)

The Syrian general had given orders to slay only the king of Israel—Ahab.

> But the king of Syria commanded his thirty and two
> captains that had rule over his chariots, saying, Fight
> neither with small nor great, save only with the king of
> Israel. (1 Kings 22:31)

Jehoshaphat was not injured, although he wore his royal clothes.

And it came to pass, when the captains of the chariots saw
Jehoshaphat, that they said, Surely it is the king of Israel.
And they turned aside to fight against him: and
Jehoshaphat cried out. And it came to pass, when the
captains of the chariots perceived that it was not the king
of Israel, that they turned back from pursuing him.
(1 Kings 22:32, 33)

While war steeds neighed and war chariots rumbled and
shields clashed on shields and arrows whizzed and spears were
thrown and swords were wielded, a death-carrying arrow, shot by
an aimless and nameless archer, found the crack in Ahab's armor.

And a certain man drew a bow at a venture, and smote
the king of Israel between the joints of the harness:
wherefore he said unto the driver of his chariot, Turn
thine hand, and carry me out of the host; for I am
wounded. And the battle increased that day: and the king
was stayed up in his chariot against the Syrians, and died
at even: and the blood ran out of the wound into the
midst of the chariot. . . . And one washed the chariot in
the pool of Samaria; and the dogs licked up his blood; and
they washed his armour, *according unto the word of the
Lord which he spake.* (1 Kings 22:34, 35, 38)

Thus we learn that no man can evade God's laws with impu-
nity. All of God's laws are their own executioners. They have
strange penalties annexed. Stolen waters are sweet. But every
ounce of sweetness makes a pound of nausea. Nature keeps books
pitilessly. Man's credit with her is good. But Nature collects. And
there is no land to which you can flee and escape her bailiffs.
Every day her bloodhounds track down the men and women who
owe her.

But what about Jezebel? Did her payday come? Yes—after
twenty years. After Ahab's death, after the dogs had licked his
blood, she virtually ruled the kingdom. But I think that she went
into the temple of Baal on occasions and prayed her god Baal to
protect her from Elijah's hounds.

Elijah had been taken home to heaven without the touch of
the deathdew upon his brow. Elisha had succeeded him.

And Elisha the prophet called one of the children of the
prophets, and said unto him, Gird up thy loins, and take

this box of oil in thine hand, and go to Ramoth-gilead:
And when thou comest thither, look out there Jehu the
son of Jehoshaphat the son of Nimshi, and go in, and
make him arise up from among his brethren, and carry
him to an inner chamber; then take the box of oil and
pour it on his head and say, Thus saith the Lord, I have
anointed thee king over Israel. Then open the door and
flee, and tarry not. So the young man, even the young
man the prophet, went to Ramoth-gilead. And when he
came, behold, the captains of the host were sitting; and he
said, I have an errand to thee, O captain. And Jehu said,
Unto which of all us? And he said, To thee, O captain.
And he arose, and went into the house; and he poured
the oil on his head, and said unto him, Thus saith the
Lord God of Israel, I have anointed thee king over the
people of the Lord, even over Israel. And thou shalt smite
the house of Ahab thy master, that I may avenge the
blood of My servants the prophets, and the blood of all
the servants of the Lord, at the hand of Jezebel. . . . And I
will make the house of Ahab like the house of Jeroboam
the son of Nebat, and like the house of Baasha the son of
Ahijah: And the dogs shall eat Jezebel in the portion of
Jezreel, and there shall be none to bury her. And he
opened the door, and fled. (2 Kings 9:1-7, 9, 10)

Jehu was just the man for such an occasion—furious in his
anger, rapid in his movements, unscrupulous, yet zealous to up-
hold the law of Moses.

Then Jehu came forth to the servants of his lord: and one
said unto him, Is all well? wherefore came this mad fellow
to thee? And he said unto them, Ye know the man, and
his communication. And they said, It is false; tell us now.
And he said, Thus and thus spake he to me saying, Thus
saith the Lord, I have anointed thee king of Israel. Then
they hasted, and took every man his garment, and put it
under him on the top of the stairs, and blew with
trumpets, saying, Jehu is king. (2 Kings 9:11-13)

Mounting his chariot, commanding and taking with him a
company of his most reliable soldiers, furiously did he drive nearly sixty miles to Jezreel.

So Jehu rode in a chariot, and went to Jezreel; for Joram lay there. And Ahaziah king of Judah was come down to see Joram. And there stood a watchman on the tower in Jezreel, and he spied the company of Jehu as he came, and said, I see a company. And Joram said, Take an horseman, and send to meet them, and let him say, Is it peace? So there went one on horseback to meet him, and said, Thus saith the king, Is it peace? And Jehu said, What hast thou to do with peace? turn thee behind me. And the watchman told, saying, The messenger came to them, but he cometh not again. Then he sent out a second on horseback, which came to them, and said, Thus saith the king, Is it peace? And Jehu answered, What hast thou to do with peace? turn thee behind me. And the watchman told, saying, He came even unto them, and cometh not again: and the driving is like the driving of Jehu the son of Nimshi; for he driveth furiously. And Joram said, Make ready. And his chariot was made ready. And Joram king of Israel and Ahaziah king of Judah went out, each in his chariot, and they went out against Jehu, and met him in the portion of Naboth the Jezreelite. And it came to pass, when Joram saw Jehu, that he said, Is it peace, Jehu? And he answered, What peace, so long as the whoredoms of thy mother Jezebel and her witchcrafts are so many? And Joram turned his hands, and fled, and said to Ahaziah, There is teachery, O Ahaziah. And Jehu drew a bow with his full strength, and smote Jehoram between his arms, and the arrow went out at his heart, and he sunk down in his chariot. Then said Jehu to Bidkar his captain, Take up, and cast him in the portion of the field of Naboth the Jezreelite: for remember how that, when I and thou rode together after Ahab his father, the Lord laid this burden upon him; surely I have seen yesterday the blood of Naboth, and the blood of his sons, saith the Lord; and I will requite thee in this plat, saith the Lord. Now therefore take and cast him into the plat of ground, according to the word of the Lord. (2 Kings 9:16-26)

"And when Jehu was come to Jezreel, Jezebel heard of it." Pause! Who is Jehu? He is the one who, twenty years before the events of this chapter from which we quote, rode down with Ahab to take Naboth's vineyard, the one who throughout those twenty years never forgot those withering words of terrible denunciation which Elijah spoke. And who is Jezebel? Oh! The very same who wrote the letters and had Naboth put to death. And what is Jezreel? The place where Naboth had his vineyard and where Naboth died, his life pounded out by stones in the hands of ruffians. "And when Jehu was come to Jezreel, Jezebel heard of it; and she painted her face, and tired her head, and looked out at a window."

Just here I think of what the poet Leslie Savage Clark wrote:

From the palace casement she looked down,
   Queenly, scornful, proud,
And watched with cold indifferent eyes
   The weary ragged crowd.

   Of the wage of sin she never thought,
   Nor that a crown might fall. . . .
Nor did she note the hungry dogs
   Skulking along the wall.

And as Jehu, the new king by the will and word of the Lord, entered in at the gate, she asked: "Had Zimri peace who slew his master?" And Jehu lifted up his face to the window and said, "Who is on my side? who? And there looked out to him two or three eunuchs. And he said, Throw her down" (2 Kings 9:30-33).

These men put their strong men's fingers into her soft feminine flesh and picked her up, tired head and all, painted face and all, bejeweled fingers and all, skirts and all—and threw her down. Her body hit the street and burst open. Some of the blood splattered on the legs of Jehu's horses, dishonoring them. Some of her blood splattered on the walls of the city, disgracing them.

And Jehu drove his horses and chariot over her. There she lies, twisting in death agony in the street. Her body is crushed by the chariot wheels. On her white bosom are the black cresent-shapes of horses' hoofs. She is hissing like an adder in the fire. Jehu drove away and left her there.

And when he was come in he did eat and drink, and said, Go, see now this cursed woman, and bury her: for she is a king's daughter. And they went to bury her: but they found no more of her than the skull, and the feet, and the palms of her hands. (2 Kings 9:34, 35)

God Almighty saw to it that the hungry dogs despised the brains that conceived the plot that took Naboth's life. God Almighty saw to it that the mangy lean dogs of the back alleys despised the hands that wrote the plot that took Naboth's life. God Almighty saw to it that the lousy dogs which ate carrion despised the feet that walked in Baal's courts and then in Naboth's vineyard.

These soldiers of Jehu went back to Jehu and said: "We went to bury her, O king, but the dogs had eaten her!"

And Jehu replied:

This is the word of the Lord, which he spake by his
servant Elijah the Tishbite, saying, In the portion of Jezreel
shall dogs eat the flesh of Jezebel. And the carcass of
Jezebel shall be as dung upon the face of the field in the
portion of Jezreel; so that they shall not say, This is
Jezebel. (2 Kings 9:36, 37)

Thus perished a female demon, the most infamous queen who ever wore a royal diadem.

"Payday Someday!" God said it—and it was done! Yes, and from this we learn the power and certainty of God in carrying out His own retributive providence, that men might know that His justice slumbereth not. Even though the mill of God grinds slowly, it grinds to powder.

Yes, the judgments of God often have heels and travel slowly. But they always have iron hands and crush completely.

And when I see Ahab fall in his chariot and when I see the dogs eating Jezebel by the walls of Jezreel, I say, as the Scripture saith: "O that thou hadst hearkened to my commandments; then had thy peace been as a river, and thy righteousness as the waves of sea" (Isaiah 48:18). And as I remember that the gains of ungodliness are weighted with the curse of God, I ask you: "Wherefore do ye spend money for that which is not bread? and your labour for that which satisfieth not?" (Isaiah 55:2).

And the only way I know for any man or woman on earth to escape the sinner's payday on earth and the sinner's hell beyond—making sure of the Christian's payday on earth and the Christian's heaven beyond the Christian's payday—is through Christ Jesus, who took the sinner's place upon the cross, becoming for all sinners all that God must judge, that sinners through faith in Christ Jesus might become all that God cannot judge.

Herbert Lockyer, Sr.
1886-1984

Dr. Herbert Lockyer was born in England and was converted when he was eighteen years old after hearing an actor, Spencer Johnson, give his testimony. Lockyer enrolled in the Bible Training Institute of Glasgow, after which he spent many years as an evangelist preaching in the halls and tents throughout the mining and ship-building towns of the Scottish Lowlands.

Dr. James M. Gray, president of Moody Bible Institute of Chicago, invited Dr. Lockyer to visit the United States for a preaching mission in 1936. This led to seventeen years of Bible conference ministry in Great Britain and the United States. During this period he preached over seven thousand times.

When sixty-five, Lockyer retired to a writing ministry and for the next twenty-seven years gave the world over fifty books, some of which have been translated into Chinese, Spanish, Dutch, and Norwegian.

One of his favorite sermons was "Other Little Ships."

Other Little Ships

". . . And there were also with him other little ships."
(Mark 4:36)

The narrative from which the title of this meditation is taken abounds with so much of interest that one could easily pause to expound its broad and beautiful outline. You have the crowded seashore—the eager listeners drinking in the blessed words of the Lord Jesus—His retreat into a boat in which, weary and tired, He fell asleep—the raging storm and wave-beaten ship—the frightened disciples—and amidst all the turmoil, the sleeping, tranquil Christ.

Then follow the waking of our Lord and His rebuke of the storm and winds—His rebuke of the disciples for their little faith—and, last of all, the ever-deepening gratitude and admiration of the disciples for their omnipotent Lord and Master.

Such a thrilling sea story bids one linger, but we must hasten on to discover the significance of this sweet, simple, unpretentious phrase—"other little ships." With an eye for details, Mark alone records this fact in connection with the miracle of Christ's calming of the tempest. May the Holy Spirit reveal to us something of the pregnant truth these words contain (Mark 4:36)!

Life's Common Experiences

Out upon that Galilean sea those disciples thought that their ship was the only one in danger; that they only were battling against the storm, trying their best to keep afloat. But Mark reminds us, as probably he reminded his friends, that they were not alone upon that angry sea. Other ships were out on the foamy deep as well as their own boat. Thus the experience, although dark and discomfiting, was not singular but similar, for others had encountered the same troublesome waves and boisterous winds.

This was the lesson Elijah learned as he lived and prophesied in dark times (1 Kings 19). Israel had forsaken God, slain the prophets, despised and destroyed the altars, followed after idols. And the prophet, smitten with grief and a sense of loneliness, cried out in deep anguish, "I, even I only am left." God, however, had to remind him that he was not alone, but that there were "other little ships," others who were as true as Elijah. "I have left me seven thousand in Israel, all the knees which have not bowed unto Baal, and every mouth which hath not kissed him."

And this is the lesson each of us comes to learn as we are carried over the turbulent waters of life. We have our days of sunshine, and how we revel in their light and splendor. Suddenly, however, we encounter the storms and squalls. The howling wind descends and whips the waves into fury. The sun's face is hid, and in a darkness that can be felt we cry out for deliverance. Our complaint is, how heavy "our" burden—how sharp "our" sorrows—how fierce "our" storm! Surely we are alone in our grief. Can there be any anguish like unto ours?

Then we look around the heaving sea only to discern through the mist and foam others who are bravely sailing through the rough elements. The experiences of life, we discover, are after all similar and commonplace. While we may think of our craft, seeing it is our own, let us not forget the other little ships displaying greater courage and bravery because of their greater frailty and exposure.

When Robert Louis Stevenson was a child he would lie awake at night, and racked with coughing would pray either for sleep or morning. At times his devoted nurse, "Faithful Commie," who taught him the Shorter Catechism, would lift him out of bed and, carrying him to the window, would show him one or two lit-up windows in the dark line in Queen Street, Edinburgh. They would tell one another that there might be other sick boys with their nurses in those lighted rooms, waiting even as they were, for the morning. And, records R. L. Stevenson, "She was more patient than I, supposed an angel." Early in life he learned about the other little ships.

Now let us see how we can apply the teaching of Mark's descriptive phrase to ourselves.

Take Temptation!

It may be that your life is open to the attacks of the Devil. He is forever slinging his darts at you. Your circumstances or temperament or heredity mark you for his constant assaults. And when he is like some veritable bloodhound on your track, you feel as if you are alone in the wilderness of temptation. Then the Word of God comes to you with its withering rebuke and yet its consoling grace: "There hath no temptation taken you but such as is common to man" (1 Corinthians 10:13). You discover others in the fierce conflict besides yourself. You are reminded that you are not alone but that the Master Himself was tempted in all points like as you are.

Take Sin!

The same principle is true in respect to human failure. We are not alone in our sin, for "all have sinned." Perhaps you have fallen as low as it is possible to fall; yet others have sounded the depth of degradation. The worst sinner has been saved in the person of Paul, who declared that he was the chief of sinners; so there is hope for you. Others were once on the dunghill but are now among princes. Lives, once as ships with broken sails and at the mercy of the waves of passion, are now stately vessels. Others have been saved. Let God do the same for you!

Take Trial!

Some there are who set out upon the voyage of life with great and noble ambition. As they pushed out from the shore with their frail craft, the morning was so fair. They anticipated nothing save a pleasant and prosperous journey, but as they reached the open sea, dark clouds crept over the sun—the howling winds rose—the storm broke, filling the boat with tempest-driven waves, until it seemed as if their little craft would sink. Disappointment clouded the sky, plans and ambitions were ripped to pieces, and with a boat well-nigh derelict the cry rent the air, "Carest thou not that we perish?"

And then, and blessed be the moment, other little ships are discovered—other lives passing through similar trials and encountering the same storm. It was such a discovery that came to Mrs.

Gladstone, the wife of W. E. Gladstone. A few hours after the death of her illustrious, noble husband, she was found in the home of a poor woman whose husband had just been killed in a neighboring coal mine. That famous politician's wife had found another little ship.

Take Death!

God does not deny us our tears. Jesus wept over a grave. But it is a sin to grieve over the departure of a loved one as if no one else had ever lost a friend. Have you said, "Good-bye"? So have others. Others weep and mourn—gaze into the shadows—sit and look at vacant chairs. You must not think that your little ship is the only one occupying all the sea and that you are breasting the waves alone. Why, the sea is full of death-laden ships! "There was not a house where there was not one dead."

After the death of Prince Albert, the heart of Queen Victoria the Good was crushed with grief. The days following his death were days of unspeakable sadness. The Queen, however, was not so wrapped up in her own grief as not to feel the sorrows of others. Her first public words after the Prince's death formed an expression of tenderest sympathy sent to the wives and children of some two hundred men who were killed in the Hartley Colliery disaster in 1862. Thus a Queen learned that there were other little ships.

The Blessings of Consideration

And, further, Mark would have us consider the advantage of thinking of others. The consciousness of those other little ships out upon the same sea would have lessened the sense of the disciples' need and reduced the weight of their own distress. Their cry for deliverance would not have been so selfish if they had considered others battling against the same storm. Thinking of others is always a help to ourselves. Whenever we think of our own trouble to the exclusion of the grief of others, our burden is always magnified and our cross ten times heavier than it really is.

Thinking of Others Inspires Unselfishness!

Instead of centering all pity and compassion of others upon ourselves, we should think of our neighbors who deserve a share of fellow-feeling, making us wondrous kind. And we are not perfect until, saved from self-pity, we find joy in thinking of others. Alas! we can be guilty of selfishness even in the tears we shed and in trials we bear.

Thinking of Others Begets Sacrifice!

When we sink our personal griefs in the consciousness of other suffering hearts, we not only help them bear their burden, we also take the sharp sting out of our own bitter experience. Thinking of others produces sacrifice whereby fellow-sufferers are enriched. Thus our grief ennobles our own life and enriches others.

Do you think your life is of no account? Are you sometimes depressed by the obscurity of your sphere? Well, let Christ into your ship. Make Him the Pilot of your craft. Allow Him to calm your troubled conscience and settle your fear, and then with a soul as tranquil as a lake go out upon the tempest-driven sea and amid the foam determine to lead some other little ship into the haven of peace. And if you make this work your passion, what is left of life will take on a different hue, and you will come to the end of your days realizing that you have not lived in vain.

Yes, and remember, will you, that God so often permits personal chastisement not merely for the development of our own character, but that our sorrows might make us a blessing to others who have similar trials. Often we meet Christ in the storms of life and in despair cry out for peace of heart and solace of mind, only to go out and discover other wave-beaten ships whose needs are just as great. It was thus Mrs. Josephine Butler's tragic loss of a daughter that led her to dedicate her life for the salvation of young womanhood. Such a noble woman learned the ministry of a bleeding heart.

Thinking of Others Emulates the Divine Example!

Jesus was ever thinking of others. "Others!" were His life's passion and constant incentive. The thought of others in their dire need forced Him out of heaven into a sinful world. He flung His own life away in order that He might save others. "He saved others, Himself He did not save." Oh, what self-forgetfulness is herewith portrayed! And after nineteen hundred years of soul-saving work, there are still others He must save. God save us from our self-centeredness. Let us help the Savior to rescue the other tempest-driven ships!

The Universal Christ

It is Mark alone who records the fact that those other little ships were "with Jesus." As the Master taught in the boat manned by the apostolic crew, probably interested onlookers, anxious to get nearer Christ's person and to have a more favorable position from which they might listen to His discourses, took to their boats. Then quickly a little fleet gathered around the Savior.

Yet the disciples enjoyed a privilege the other little ships were deprived of. It was into their ship the Master entered, and in which He slept and performed His miracle. Still, if the other ships were denied His person, they all participated in His peace and power. Being all around the Sacred One, they all shared in the tranquillity He made possible. When He stilled the storm and calmed the sea, He did so not merely for His disciples but for all the storm-tossed vessels around.

Christ was human when that miracle was performed and could not therefore be in more than one place at a time. Now, by His Spirit He can fill every life willing to give Him room. The miracle that evening was not for one ship but for all. In like manner the divine provision of the cross is for all. Grace knows no favoritism. All Christ has is pardon, peace, and power for all. All is for all!

And so, my friend, if you have found Jesus and made Him the Master of your boat, will you realize that He yearns to be the Pilot of every other vessel and that He wants you to help Him realize His plan?

If through the billows of temptation, sorrow, disappointment, and death you have found the miracle-working Lord and have entered into the secret of the peace, do not keep the treasure to yourself; remember others! Do not be selfish with what you have and know of Christ, but take Him out to others upon life's tempestuous sea. Finding other little ships about to sink, say to them, as they battle against troubled circumstances, "Friend, give Jesus the helm! Make Him the Pilot of your life." Then it will be true of others even as it was of you—"He maketh the storm a calm so that the waves thereof are still. Then are they glad because they be quieted. So bringeth He them into their desired haven."

Paul E. Little
1928-1975

Paul Little was born in Philadelphia and educated at the Wharton School of Finance, Wheaton College, Chicago Lutheran Seminary, and New York University.

At the time of his death in an automobile accident, he was assistant to the president of Inter-Varsity Christian Fellowship and associate professor of evangelism in the World School of Missions of Trinity Evangelical Divinity School. He was also associate director of the program of the 1974 Lausanne Conference on World Evangelism.

Little's ministry was especially effective on the university campuses across the United States and Canada. His books Know What You Believe, Know Why You Believe, and How to Give Away Your Faith still have a wide ministry on the campuses as well as elsewhere.

"Affirming the Will of God" was preached at the Urbana Missionary Conference.

Affirming
the Will of God

Suppose for a moment that the Lord Jesus Christ were to grant you the answer to one question—any question you wanted to ask. What would that question be?

My guess is that it would probably relate in some way to knowing God's will for your life. After all, to a committed Christian this is really the only thing that counts. Our peace and satisfaction depend on knowing that God is guiding us. And the absence of that certainty leaves us fearful and restless.

But we have a problem because we are confused about what the will of God is in the first place. And unless we are clear about that, we really cannot make much progress. Most people speak of God's will as something you have or don't have. "Have you discovered God's will for your life?" they ask each other. What they usually mean is, "Have you discovered God's 'blueprint' for your life?" But the fact is that God seldom reveals an entire blueprint. So if you are looking for that blueprint in its entirety, you are likely to be disappointed. What God does most frequently reveal, however, is the next step in His will. But this leads us into the fuller question of what exactly God's will is.

It is important to understand at the outset that God has a plan and purpose for your life. This is one of the sensational aspects of being a Christian—to know that your life can be tied into God's plan and purpose not only for time but for eternity. Paul writes, "For we are his (God's) workmanship, created in Christ Jesus for good works, which God prepared beforehand, that we should walk in them" (Ephesians 2:10). David, in Psalm 37:23, says, "The steps of a man are from the Lord, and he establishes him in whose way he delights." And in Acts 13:2 we read: "While they were worshiping the Lord and fasting, the Holy

137

Spirit said, 'Set apart for me Barnabas and Saul for the work to which I have called them.' "

Not only does God have a plan for us, but He has promised to reveal it to us. In Psalm 73:24 David says of God: "Thou dost guide me with thy counsel, and afterward thou wilt receive me to glory." In Psalm 32:8 God promises, "I will instruct you and teach you the way you should go; I will counsel (or guide) you with my eye upon you."

Finally, those classic verses, Proverbs 3:5, 6, two of the most compact verses on guidance in the whole Bible, say, "Trust in the Lord with all your heart, and do not rely on your own insight. In all your ways acknowledge him, and he will make straight your paths."

Two Aspects of God's Will

There are two aspects to God's will. The first is that aspect of His will and His plan which has already been revealed in His Word and which applies to every Christian. The second aspect involves those decisions in which God has given no specific instructions.

Has it ever struck you that the vast majority of the will of God for your life has already been revealed in the Bible? That is the crucial thing to grasp.

There are many positive commands. For instance, we are commanded by our Lord to go into all the world and preach the gospel to every creature. We know it is the will of God (from Romans 8:29) that we are to be conformed to the image of Christ. If you want more details, read the book of James, list all the specific commands there, and you will have a good start on the will of God for your life.

Scripture also contains many negative commands. God tells us in unmistakable terms in 2 Corinthians 6:14 that we are not to be unequally yoked together with unbelievers. This means, among other things, that a Christian is never to marry an unbeliever. Are any of you praying for guidance about whether you should marry a non-Christian? Save your breath.

The late A. W. Tozer pointed out that we should never seek guidance on what God has already forbidden. Nor should we ever seek guidance in the areas where He has already said yes and given us a command. Then, Tozer suggests, in most other things God has no preference.

God really does not have a great preference whether you have steak or chicken. He is not desperately concerned about whether you wear a green shirt or a blue shirt. In many areas of life, God invites us to consult our own sanctified preferences. When we are pleased, God is pleased. That is a wonderful thing to know, isn't it?

Then Tozer points out that there are, on the other hand, areas in which we need special guidance. These are the areas of life where there is no specific statement like, "Thou, John Jones, shalt be an engineer in Cincinnati," or, "Thou, Mary Smith, shalt marry Fred Grottenheimer." No verse in the Bible will give you that kind of detail in your life. But God has promised us special guidance in these areas. The Lord spoke to the prophet Isaiah: "I am the Lord your God, who teaches you to profit, who leads you in the way you should go" (Isaiah 48:17).

By recognizing the two aspects of God's will—namely, what is already specifically revealed in His Word and what is not—we get away from the static concept of the blueprint. The will of God is not like a magic package let down out of heaven by a string, a package we grope after in desperation and hope sometime in the future to clasp to our hearts.

The will of God is far more like a scroll that unrolls every day. In other words, God has a will for you and me today and tomorrow and the next day and the day after that. Now it may well be that a decision we make this week or next week will commit us for three months, or two years, or five or ten years, or for a lifetime. But the fact still remains that the will of God is something to be discerned and to be lived out each day of our lives. It is not something to be grasped as a package once for all. Our call, therefore, is basically not to follow a plan or a blueprint, or to go to a place or take up a work, but rather to follow the Lord Jesus Christ. When we realize this, then we will begin to sense something of its dynamic.

Prerequisites for Special Guidance

Now, after understanding something of the two aspects of the will of God, we need to look at the prerequisites for knowing the will of God in the unspecified areas of our lives.

One prerequisite is *to be a child of God.* One day some people asked Jesus directly, "What must we do, to be doing the works of

God?" And Jesus answered specifically and clearly, "This is the work (or the will) of God, that you believe in him whom he has sent" (John 6:29). We must first come to Jesus in a commitment of faith to Him as Savior and Lord. Then we are God's children and can be guided by Him as our Father. The Lord said in John 10:3, "He calls his own sheep by name and leads them out."

The second prerequisite is *to obey, at least in the desires of our hearts, the will of God in those areas where we know what it is.* What is the point of God's guiding us in areas in which He has not been specific when we are apparently unconcerned about areas in which He is specific? Mark Twain once wryly observed, "It's not the parts of the Bible I don't understand that bother me, it's the parts I do understand." Perhaps this is the problem for some of us now. We need to begin to obey in those specific areas.

We know, for example, that we ought to be meeting with the Lord every day in prayer. "But," you say, "you don't know my schedule. I've got a heavy course load this year. And yatita, yatita." All of us have twenty-four hours equally. It is merely a matter of setting priorities. If you are going to meet with God every day, it means you decide when you are going to bed, when you will get up, and when you are going to study. You may have vaguely wanted to witness to that fellow or girl down the hall. Then decide when you are going to do it. Attempt to contact that friend to see if there is any openness to the gospel.

What are the areas of the will of God that you already understand? To what extent are you acting on that understanding?

The third prerequisite, and I think the most crucial, is *to be willing to accept the will of God in these unspecified areas of our lives before knowing what it is.* In other words, we must accept God's will in advance. For most of us, I suspect, this is where the real problem lies. If we are really honest, we would have to admit that our attitude is, "Lord, show me what Your will is so I can decide whether it fits in with what I have in mind." In essence we are saying, "Just lift the curtain a minute and let me see so I can decide whether I want to do it or not. Show me whether I'm to be married or not. Show me where in the world You want me to be and what You want me to do. If it's Palm Beach or Laguna Beach or Honolulu or some wonderful place like that, then maybe I'll consider it a little more seriously."

If we stop to analyze this attitude, we should be shocked, for what we are doing is insulting God. We are saying, "I think I know better than You, God, what will make me happy. I don't trust You. If I let You run my life, You're going to shortchange me." Have you ever felt like that? It is a solemn thing to realize.

We have the tragic, mistaken idea that we must choose between doing what we want to do and being happy, and doing what God wants us to do and being miserable. We think that the will of God is some horrible thing which he sort of shoves under our nose and demands, "All right! Are you willing, are you willing?" If we could just get out from under His clammy hands, we could really swing.

Nothing could be further from the truth. Such notions are a slur on the character of God. So many of us see God as a kind of celestial Scrooge who peers over the balcony of heaven trying to find anybody who is enjoying life. And when He spots a happy person, He yells, "Now cut that out!" That concept of God should make us shudder because it's blasphemous!

We need to have the tremendous truth of Romans 8:32 deeply planted in our hearts: "He who did not spare his own Son but gave him up for us all, will he not also give us all things with him?" If you can get hold of that verse, memorize it, meditate on it, and allow it to get hold of you, you will have solved 90 percent of your problem with desire for the will of God, because you will realize the God who loved us enough to die for us when we did not care that much for Him is not about to shortchange us in life when we give our lives to Him. As Oswald Hoffman of the "Lutheran Hour" has put it, "Having given us the package, do you think God will deny us the ribbon?"

Think of it in human terms for a moment. I have two children, a girl Debbie, and a son Paul. (We call him Small Paul, Small Paul Little. When you realize that in Greek *paulos* means small, it is the ultimate in redundancy.) When my children come to me and say, "Daddy, I love you," do you think I respond by saying, "Ah, children, that's just what I've been waiting to hear. Into the closet for three weeks. Bread and water. I've just been waiting for you to tell me you love me so I can make your life miserable!" Do you think that is the way I respond? Of course not. They could get anything they wanted out of me at that point.

Do you think that God is any less loving than a human father? God's love far transcends any love that we as humans express. The Bible is constantly drawing contrasts between human love and activity and our Heavenly Father's love. "If you then, who are evil," Jesus says in Luke 11:13, "know how to give good gifts to your children, how much more will the heavenly Father give the Holy Spirit to those who ask him!"

When we come to God and say, "I love You, and I'm prepared to do Your will whatever You want me to do," we can be sure that God is not going to make us miserable. Rather He rejoices and fits our lives into His pattern for us, into that place where He, in His omniscience and love, knows we will fit hand in glove. The One who is our Creator, who made us, who knows us better than we will ever know ourselves, is the one we are talking to. He knows the end from the beginning.

I love the third verse of the hymn "Still Will We Trust":

Choose for us, God, nor let our weak preferring
Cheat us of good Thou hast for us designed:
Choose for us, God; Thy wisdom is unerring.
And we are fools and blind.

God's will is not loathsome. It is the greatest thing in all of life to get hold of. There is no greater joy or satisfaction than to be in the center of the will of God and know it. Jim Elliot, one of the five martyrs in Ecuador in 1956, wrote of the sheer joy of doing the will of God, as recorded in his biography, *Shadow of the Almighty.*

In the light of the character of God and considering the experience of people who have known him, I dislike intensely the phrase "surrender to the will of God." To me that implies kicking, struggling, screaming. It is like saying, "There is no other way out. I'm running, but I'm caught. I've got to collapse and surrender. It's all over. I give up."

I far prefer the term, "affirm the will of God." If we had any sense at all, every one of us would affirm God's will with confidence and with joy and with deep satisfaction.

This third prerequisite is therefore crucial. It involves eliminating any holdout areas in your life—a relationship, an ambition, a qualification. No more saying, "I'll go anywhere, Lord, but . . ." or "I'll go and do anything, but it's got to be with so-and-so." Rather we will say, "Lord, You've created me and I belong to You. Even when I was a rebel against You, You loved me enough to die for me. Everything I am and have belongs to You. I'm not my own; I'm bought with a price—the precious blood of Christ—and I consciously and joyfully commit myself to You. Do with me as You choose." And when we come to that place, we will be able to say with Paul, and mean it in the depths of our hearts, "To me to live is Christ."

We must first, then, understand what the will God is. Then we must be prepared to accept the prerequisites for knowing it in those areas about which the Bible is not specific. And in the third place we need to understand how, in fact, God guides in the areas in which he has not been specific.

Principles of Guidance

First, in addition to specific commands, *there are principles in the Word of God which may have direct implications for our situation.*

Several years ago I knew a girl who had signed a contract to teach. In August she received another offer from a school closer to where she wanted to live. So she broke the original contract. Had she acted on the Biblical principle in Psalm 15:4, where God says that He is pleased with a person who swears to his own hurt and does not change, she would not have done that. The department chairman who told me about the Christian girl's action said her justification was "I have a peace about it," and he commented rather sardonically, "Isn't that lovely? She's got the peace and I've got the pieces." I believe that girl missed the will of God. She violated a principle which, if she had been alert and had applied it to her situation, would have given her clear guidance in this specific detail of her life. God guides, then, through His Word and its principles.

Second, *God guides us in prayer as we ask Him to show us His will.* At the Urbana Convention in 1948, Dr. Norton Sterrett asked, "How many of you who are concerned about the will of God spend five minutes a day asking Him to show you His will?" It was as if somebody had grabbed me by the throat. At that time I was an undergraduate concerned about what I should do when I graduated from the university. I was running around campus— going to this meeting, reading that book, trying to find some- body's little formula (1, 2, 3, 4 and a bell rings)—and I was frustrated out of my mind trying to figure out the will of God. I was doing everything but getting into the presence of God and asking Him to show me.

May I ask the same question: Do you spend even five minutes a day specifically asking God to show you His will?

As we pray, God often gives us a conviction by the Holy Spirit which deepens, despite new information, to an increasing sense of rightness or oughtness about a course of action. This is quite different from the "gung ho" emotion which prods us today to get on a plane to Hong Kong, and tomorrow to move into Chicago, and the next day to paddle a canoe up the Amazon, and each day after to go in a different direction. When the Holy Spirit begins to move in our hearts, one conviction deepens and, while we recognize other situations, we sense that this is the will of God for us.

Third, *God guides and directs us through circumstances.* Here, however, we must be particularly on guard. Most of us tend to make circumstances 99 percent of the guidance. But they are only one of the factors in guidance. Furthermore, we must view circumstances from God's perspective and values; they may be more of a guide negatively than positively.

For instance, if you think that God is leading you to go to graduate school in engineering, but you cannot get into any school in this country or abroad, it may be fairly clear that God does not want you in engineering school. On the other hand, the fact that you are accepted into three engineering schools does not necessarily mean that God wants you to go into engineering. There are other factors to consider.

You may graduate from the university and have fifteen job offers, but that does not necessarily mean that God wants you to accept any of them. He may have a prior claim on your life that will involve your going into a far corner of the earth. You may even be called of God to do something that the average non-Christian, who sees nothing but the visible world bounded by the cradle and the grave, would consider a tragic waste of time and talent.

Although circumstances per se are not a guide, God may use them. A summer trip abroad may show you whether and where God wants you to go overseas. In this jet age every student ought to consider the possibility of spending a semester or summer in some other culture. On the other hand, as a result of study and circumstances, God might confirm a call to you here in the States.

Familiarize yourself with the needs of the world. While it is quite true that in itself a need is not a call, the overwhelming needs everywhere cannot be ignored. The old illustration of a log carried by nine men on one end and three women on the other may be trite and corny, but it has a profound point: Which end of the log will you help carry? It is a fact that 90 percent of full-time Christian workers are in parts of the world which have 10 percent of the world's population; 10 percent of them are in population centers comprising 90 percent of the world's population. Surely this is not the will of God since He has already told us in His Word that He wants every person to hear the gospel. Millions of people have never heard the gospel at all.

In his leaflet *Don't Wait for the Macedonians,* David Howard asks, "Why should anyone seek more specific direction to serve the Lord overseas than He does to serve in any other capacity or location? It may well be that we should make every effort to go overseas unless God clearly calls us to stay home, rather than the reverse. And as you make the effort, as you begin to move, God will guide. God can close doors very easily. But, as the old saying goes, you can't steer a parked car; you can't pilot a moored ship."

God will also guide you through circumstances as you get involved in evangelism where you are. It is foolish to think of traveling to some other part of the world if God isn't already using you in the lives of people around you now.

Trust God to give you a solid friendship with at least one person from overseas. Ask God to enable you to share the greatest thing in all of life—the love of Jesus—and to articulate the gospel to your friends. If you are able to get through to American, Canadian, and international students on your own campus, God may then put a fire in your bones that will move you to some other part of the world.

Fourth, *God guides us through the counsel of other Christians who are fully committed to the will of God and who know us well.* This is one of the most neglected dimensions of guidance today.

It sounds terribly spiritual to say "God led me," but I am always suspicious of a person who implies that he has a *personal* pipeline to God. When no one else senses that what the person suggests is the will of God, then we had better be careful. God has been blamed for the most outlandish things by people who have confused their own inverted pride with God's will.

Occasionally I hear of a guy who, in the name of spiritual guidance, rushes up to a girl and says, "Susie, God has told me you're to marry me." I have news for him. If that is the will of

God, then Susie is going to get the message too. If she does not, somebody's radar is jammed, and it's not hard to tell whose.

Are you wondering about marriage? Whether God might use you in an overseas situation? Talk to some of your mature Christian friends, your pastor, elders in your church, and others who know you and are themselves concerned for the will of God. Their counsel may be invaluable. It is true that sometimes we get mixed counsel from Christian friends, but their advice is frequently helpful. Remember what Acts 15 records: "It has seemed good to the Holy Spirit and to us . . ." I believe God usually guides in that way—a personal conviction corroborated by friends' opinions. Don't be afraid to talk to people whom you think might give you advice you don't want to hear. You may be too emotionally involved in a situation to see it objectively and need somebody to talk straight to you so that you can be realistic in your assessments.

When all four of these factors—the Word of God, conviction that he gives us in prayer, circumstances, and the counsel of mature Christian friends—converge, it is usually a sign that God is leading and guiding us.

Common Mistakes to Avoid

Finally, I want to discuss some serious mistakes to avoid in thinking about the will of God. First, *we must not think that because we want to do something, it can't possibly be God's will.* That attitude displays a distorted concept of the character of God. We really think he is a celestial killjoy. We need to recognize the wonderful truth of Psalm 37:4: "Take delight in the Lord, and he will give you the desires of your heart." This does not mean, "Delight yourself in the Lord and He will give you a Stingray, a Cadillac, a Phi Beta Kappa key, and the whole business." What it means is that as we delight ourselves in the Lord, we come "to will with Him one will." Our will and God's will begin to coincide. The greatest joy in all our lives is to do what the Lord wants us to do and to know we are doing it. Then we can say with our Lord, "My food is to do the will of him who sent me" (John 4:34). Admittedly, we must constantly guard against self-deception, but when we really want to do the will of God and do it, we have deep joy and satisfaction.

Second, *we must not feel that every decision we make must have a subjective confirmation.* I have known people who have been paralyzed and couldn't act at all because they did not have some kind of electrifying liver-shiver about the whole thing. If you are facing an important decision in which God has not given you specific guidance, postpone the decision, if you can, until the way seems clear. But if you must decide by next Saturday and next Saturday comes and you still don't have clear guidance, then you must trust that God will guide you in the decision. After assessing all the factors, launch out in faith, saying, "Lord, as I see it, there are four equally valid possibilities in front of me. I see no particular advantage or disadvantage in any of these options. So I am going down route 3 unless You close the door. I am trusting that You won't let me make a crucial mistake."

If we do that, we can act joyfully, believing God has guided us. We don't have to spend the next twenty-four years second-guessing ourselves as to whether or not we are in the will of God. God does not play the game of mousetrap with us. He does not say, "Ha, ha. You thought that was the right lane, but it wasn't. Return to Go. Better luck next time." We must get rid of these distorted concepts of God's character. The God who loved us enough to die for us is not going to play games with our lives. We mean too much to Him. Rather, we can claim His promise, "Trust in the Lord with all your heart, and do not rely on your own insight. In all your ways acknowledge him, and he will make straight your paths" (Proverbs 3:5).

Third, *we must realize that there are often logical implications involved in the will of God.* If some things are the will of God, then a whole series of other things are automatically the will of God and we do not have to pray about them. For example, if God leads you to get married, you do not have to spend hours in prayer agonizing over whether or not it is the will of God that you should support your wife. This is painfully self-evident, and yet I have met so many people who do not seem to have grasped it. I once loaned a guy ten dollars, and he is still praying about whether he ought to pay me back.

Fourth, *we must not think that God's will is necessarily something wild and bizarre.* Many people are afraid of using their reason in determining God's will. But we must recognize that God is not the author of confusion. When the Scripture says, "Do not rely on your own insight," it does not mean to kiss your brains good-bye. Rather, the Holy Spirit illumines us and then guides our enlightened reason. It may be that He will lead us to do something that is contrary to our unenlightened reason, but the idea that His will is frequently bizarre is a very dangerous assumption.

Fifth, *we must guard very carefully against the subtle temptation to decide what we are going to do for God.* This mistake is really critical. There is a vast difference between saying, "Lord, I'm going to be a business executive (or missionary or whatever) for You," and asking, "Lord, what will You have me to do?" It sounds very spiritual to say, "I'm going to be an executive for the Lord and make money and give it to the Lord's work." Or, "I'll be a missionary for the Lord." But the Lord has not asked you to decide what you are going to be. Rather, He has invited you to be a recruit and say to the Commander-in-Chief, "Here I am. Where in the battle line do You want me?"

In this connection, be careful you are not tied too closely to your background so that you think God can use you only in the context of the training you have. God may, and probably will, lead you in the area of your training, but as George Cowan says in the booklet *Your Training or You?* God wants you more than He wants your training. I took my training in accounting and business administration, but God never led me into that field. I have been in student work since I graduated.

Sixth, *we must guard against the temptation to take Bible verses out of context to get God's will.* Some people treat the Bible as a book of magic. You have probably heard of the fellow who opened the Bible and put his finger down on the phrase, "Judas went out and hanged himself." That did not comfort him very much, so he tried again. And his finger fell on the verse, "Go thou and do likewise." That shook him terribly, so he tried it one more time, and the verse he hit on was, "And what thou doest, do quickly."

On rare occasions, God will take a verse which has no specific application to you and give you a message through it, but this is the exception rather than the rule. The basic Biblical principle is to interpret and understand the Bible in context. When this is violated, God gets blamed for all kinds of things which are merely human stupidity. I remember a British girl several years ago who was sure God was going to give her a visa for the States because a Bible verse (Isaiah 41:2) said something about God raising up a righteous man from the east. I asked her, "What about the rest of the verse that says God is going to use him to destroy people with the sword?" She didn't get a visa. God didn't fail. She did—because she violated the principle of interpreting Scripture in context.

Seventh, *we must avoid the mistake of thinking that we can be sure we are in the will of God if everything is moonlight and roses, if we have no problems or stress.* Frequently just when we take a step of obedience, the bottom falls out of everything. Then only the confidence that we are in the will of God keeps us going.

Never forget the incident recorded in Mark 4. The disciples, at the Lord's specific command, had gotten into a boat to head across the Sea of Galilee. After they took this step of obedience to the Lord, the storm broke loose and they thought they were going to lose their lives. But Jesus said to them, "Why are you afraid? Have you no faith?"

In Mark 5 Jairus came to our Lord saying, "My daughter's sick. Will you come heal her?" The Lord said He would, and Jairus' spirit soared. But on the way some lady, who had had a medical problem for twelve years and who surely could have waited another two hours, interrupted them and Jesus became involved with her. Jairus' servants came and said, "Look, don't bother him any longer. Your daughter has died." Jairus, who had done what was right—had gotten the answer from the Lord, had followed His will and obeyed—must have been crushed in bitter despair. But our Lord's words to him come to us as well in similar circumstances: "Do not fear. Only believe." The test of whether you are in the will of God is not how rosy your circumstances are, but whether you are obeying Him.

Eighth, *we must avoid the mistake of thinking a call to evangelism or missionary service is any different from a call to anything else.* Dr. Norton Sterrett, in his helpful booklet *Called by God and Sure of It*, points out that all Christians—whether as wives or husbands, electricians or lawyers, teachers or cabinetmakers—have both the privilege and the responsibility to know that they are called by God. And they also have the privilege and responsibility to know whether they are to serve in Cairo or Chicago. You don't get three more spiritual points in God's book for going overseas rather than staying in America, for being in the ministry rather than in some other form of endeavor. We have a false hierarchy of spiritual values which is not Biblical at all. Some people overseas ought to be home, and many people at home ought to be overseas.

The crucial question we all must ask ourselves is, "Am I in the will of God and sure of it?" It is not a question of fastening our spiritual seat belts and hoping we will not be swept by some emotion out of our seats into overseas service. It is not a question of taking our chances with the draft and if by some miracle it misses us, saying, "Phew, it got by me. I survived the missionary call, man, and now I can do as I please." Each of us has the privilege of discovering what God wants us to do.

Finally, I want to suggest that *each of us should avoid the mistake of thinking that if we have ever knowingly and deliberately disobeyed the Lord, we are forever thrown on the ash heap, can never do the Lord's will, and are doomed to "second best."* God has the most wonderful ways of reweaving the strands of our lives. He takes us where we are when we come to Him in confession and repentance and uses us fully again. Our disobedience did not take Him by surprise, and His grace reaches right to us.

John Mark is a good example. He seemed to have blown it when he started out on a missionary trip with Paul. At the first stop he left and headed back for Jerusalem. You will remember that Paul and Barnabas had such a hassle over whether John Mark should go with them again on the next trip that Paul and Barnabas separated. But it seems that Mark was redeemed by God and redeemed himself and later had a full and fruitful ministry which Paul commended.

When you are feeling bad and know you have sinned and blown it, remember Peter too. He denied the Lord. But our Lord took hold of him, restored him, and made him a great apostle who has given us a part of the Word of God.

God's Will for You

What is God's will for you? Realize, first, that God's will in most of its aspects is already fully revealed. Be sure you are familiar with it in the Word of God. In those areas about which He has not been specific, be assured God will guide you through His Word and its principles as you seek His face in prayer, as you view the circumstances from His point of view and seek the counsel of other Christians. Then, when you can say, "Lord, I want to do Your will more than anything else in life," and as you avoid some of the mistakes which are often based on a distortion of the character of God, you will know where in the world and how in the world God wants you to serve Him. He will show you what His will for you is today, and the next day, and the day after that.

Have you ever affirmed the will of God in your life personally? Paul, in Romans 12, invites you, "Therefore, my brothers, I implore you by God's mercy to offer your very selves to him: a living sacrifice, dedicated and fit for his acceptance, the worship offered by mind and heart. Adapt yourselves no longer to the pattern of this present world, but let your minds be remade and your whole nature thus transformed. Then you will be able to discern the will of God, and to know what is good, acceptable, and perfect" (NEB).

Francis A. Schaeffer
1912-1984

Dr. Francis A. Schaeffer was widely recognized as one of the most influential thinkers of our day. He founded L'Abri (French for "The Shelter") Fellowship, an international study center and Christian community with branches in Switzerland, England, The Netherlands, Sweden, and the U.S. Through this ministry Dr. Schaeffer came in personal contact with thousands of people searching for truth and reality in their lives. He lectured frequently in leading universities in the U.S. and abroad on the relevance of Christian truth for all of life.

Dr. Schaeffer authored twenty-three books. More than three million copies have been sold, and have been translated into more than twenty-five languages. Evangelist Billy Graham described Dr. Schaeffer as "one of the great statesmen of our generation. He spoke boldly in defense of the Bible as God's absolute truth."

"No Little People, No Little Places" is one of the sermons delivered in the chapel which serves as the worship and study center of L'Abri where Dr. Schaeffer worked for twenty-seven years. While some of his sermons are topical, many expounded Old Testament passages or some New Testament passages. Some leaned toward theology and doctrine, others toward life and practice of Christian faith. This sermon is timely for the age in which we live.

No Little People,
No Little Places

s a Christian considers the possibility of being *the Christian glorified* (a topic I discuss in *True Spirituality*), often his reaction is, "I am so limited. Surely it does not matter much whether I am walking as a creature glorified or not." Or, to put it in another way, "It is wonderful to be a Christian, but I am such a small person, so limited in talents—or energy or psychological strength or knowledge—that what I do is not really important."

The Bible, however, has quite a different emphasis: with God there are no little people.

Moses' Rod

One thing that has encouraged me, as I have wrestled with such questions in my own life, is the way God used Moses' rod, a stick of wood. Many years ago, when I was a young pastor just out of seminary, this study of the use of Moses' rod, which I called "God So Used a Stick of Wood," was a crucial factor in giving me the courage to press on.

The story of Moses' rod began when God spoke to Moses from the burning bush, telling him to go and challenge Egypt, the greatest power of his day. Moses reacted, "Who am I, that I should go unto Pharaoh, and that I should bring forth the children of Israel out of Egypt?" (Exodus 3:11), and he raised several specific objections: "They will not believe me, nor hearken unto my voice; for they will say, The Lord hath not appeared unto thee. And the Lord said unto him, What is that in thine hand? And he said, A rod" (Exodus 4:1, 2). God directed Moses' attention to the simplest thing imaginable—the staff in his own hand, a shepherd's rod, a stick of wood somewhere between three and six feet long.

Shepherds are notorious for hanging onto their staves as long as they can, just as some of us enjoy keeping walking sticks. Moses probably had carried this same staff for years. Since he had been a shepherd in the wilderness for forty years, it is entirely possible that this wood had been dead that long. Just a stick of wood—but when Moses obeyed God's command to toss it to the ground, it became a serpent, and Moses himself fled from it. God next ordered him to take it by the tail and when he did so, it became a rod again. Then God told him to go and confront the power of Egypt and meet Pharaoh face to face with this rod in his hand.

Exodus 4:20 tells us the secret of all that followed: *the rod of Moses had become the rod of God.*

Standing in front of Pharaoh, Aaron cast down this rod and it became a serpent. As God spoke to Moses and as Aaron was the spokesman of Moses (Exodus 4:16), so it would seem that Aaron used the rod of Moses which had become the rod of God. The wizards of Egypt, performing real magic through the power of the Devil (not just a stage trick through sleight of hand), matched this. Here was demonic power. But the rod of God swallowed up the other rods. This was not merely a victory of Moses over Pharaoh, but of Moses' God over Pharaoh's god and the power of the Devil behind that god.

This rod appeared frequently in the ensuing events:

> Get thee unto Pharaoh in the morning; lo, he goeth out
> unto the water; and thou shalt stand by the river's brink
> against he come; and the rod which was turned to a
> serpent shalt thou take in thine hand. And thou shalt say
> unto him, The Lord God of the Hebrews hath sent me
> unto thee, saying, Let my people go, that they may serve
> me in the wilderness; and, behold, hitherto thou wouldest
> not hear. Thus saith the Lord, In this thou shalt know
> that I am the Lord: behold, I will smite with the rod that
> is in mine hand upon the waters which are in the river,
> and they shall be turned to blood. (Exodus 7:15-17)

The rod of God indeed was in Aaron's hand (Exodus 7:17, 19, 20), and the water was putrefied, an amazing use for a mere stick of wood. In the days that followed, Moses "stretched forth his rod" and successive plagues came upon the land. After the waters no longer were blood, after seven days, there came frogs, then lice, then thunder and hail and great balls of lightning running along the ground, and then locusts (Exodus 8:1—10:15). Watch the destruction of judgment which came from a dead stick of wood that had become the rod of God.

Pharaoh's grip on the Hebrews was shaken loose, and he let the people go. But then he changed his mind and ordered his armies to pursue them. When the armies came upon them, the Hebrews were caught in a narrow place with mountains on one side of them and the sea on the other. And God said to Moses, "Lift thou up thy rod" (Exodus 14:16). What good is it to lift up a rod when one is caught in a cul-de-sac between mountains and a great body of water with the mightiest army in the world at his heels? Much good, if the rod is the rod of God. The waters divided, and the people passed through. Up to this point, the rod had been used for judgment and destruction, but now it was as much a rod of healing for the Jews as it had been a rod of judgment for the Egyptians. That which is in the hand of God can be used in either way.

Later, the rod of judgment also became a rod of supply. In Rephidim the people desperately needed water.

> And the Lord said unto Moses, Go on before the people,
> and take with thee of the elders of Israel; and thy rod,
> wherewith thou smotest the river, take in thine hand, and
> go. Behold, I will stand before thee there upon the rock in
> Horeb; and thou shalt smite the rock, and there shall
> come water out of it, that the people may drink. And
> Moses did so in the sight of the elders of Israel. (Exodus
> 17:5, 6)

It must have been an amazing sight to stand before a great rock (not a small pebble, but a face of rock such as we see here in Switzerland in the mountains) and to see a rod struck against it, and then to watch torrents of life-giving water flow out to satisfy thousands upon thousands of people and their livestock. The giver of judgment became the giver of life. It was not magic. There was nothing in the rod itself. The rod of Moses had simply become the rod of God. We too are not only to speak a word of judgment to our lost world, but are also to be a source of life.

The rod also brought military victory as it was held up. It was more powerful than the swords of either the Jews or their enemy (Exodus 17:9). In a much later incident the people revolted against Moses, and a test was established to see whom God had indeed chosen. The rod was placed before God and it budded (Numbers 17:8). Incidentally, we find out what kind of tree it had come from so long ago because it now brought forth almond blossoms.

The final use of the rod occurred when the wilderness wandering was almost over. Moses' sister Miriam had already died. Forty years had passed since the people had left Egypt; so now the rod may have been almost eighty years old. The people again needed water, and though they were now in a different place, the desert of Zin, they were still murmuring against God. So God told Moses,

> Take the rod, and gather thou the assembly together, thou, and Aaron, thy brother, and speak ye unto the rock before their eyes; and it shall give forth its water . . . and thou shalt give the congregation and their beasts drink. And Moses took the rod from before the Lord, as he commanded him. (Numbers 20:8, 9)

Moses took the rod (which verse 9 with 17:10 shows was the same one which had been kept with the ark since it had budded), and he struck the rock twice. He should have done what God had told him and only spoken with the rod in his hand, but that is another study. In spite of this, however, "water came out abundantly" (Numbers 20:11).

Consider the mighty ways in which God used a dead stick of wood. "God so used a stick of wood" can be a banner cry for each of us. Though we are limited and weak in talent, physical energy, and psychological strength, we are not less than a stick of wood. But as the rod of Moses had to become the rod of God, so that which is *me* must become the *me* of God. Then I can become useful in God's hands. The Scripture emphasizes that much can come from little if the little is truly consecrated to God. There are no little people and no big people in the true spiritual sense, but only consecrated and unconsecrated people. The problem for each of us is applying this truth to ourselves: is Francis Schaeffer the Francis Schaeffer of God?

No Little Places

But if a Christian is consecrated, does this mean he will be in a big place instead of a little place? The answer, the next step, is very important: as there are no little people in God's sight, so there are no little places. To be wholly committed to God in the place where God wants him—this is the creature glorified. In my writing and lecturing I put much emphasis on God's being the infinite reference point which integrates the intellectual problems of life. He is to be this, but He must be the reference point not only in our thinking, but in our living. This means being what He wants me to be, where He wants me to be.

Nowhere more than in America are Christians caught in the twentieth-century syndrome of size. Size will show success. If I am consecrated, there will necessarily be large quantities of people, dollars, etc. This is not so. Not only does God not say that size and spiritual power go together, but He even reverses this (especially in the teaching of Jesus) and tells us to be deliberately careful not to choose a place too big for us. We all tend to emphasize big works and big places, but all such emphasis is of the flesh. To think in such terms is simply to hearken back to the old, unconverted, egoist, self-centered Me. This attitude, taken from the world, is more dangerous to the Christian than fleshly amusement or practice. It is the flesh.

People in the world naturally want to boss others. Imagine a boy beginning work with a firm. He has a lowly place and is ordered around by everyone: Do this! Do that! Every dirty job is his. He is the last man on the totem pole, merely one of Rabbit's friends-and-relations, in Christopher Robin's terms. So one day when the boss is out, he enters the boss's office, looks around carefully to see that no one is there, and then sits down in the boss's big chair. "Someday," he says, "I'll say 'run' and they'll run." This is man. And let us say with tears that a person does not automatically abandon this mentality when he becomes a Christian. In every one of us there remains a seed of wanting to be boss, of wanting to be in control and have the word of power over our fellows.

But the Word of God teaches us that we are to have a very different mentality:

> But Jesus called them [His disciples] to him, and saith unto them, Ye know that they who are accounted to rule over

the Gentiles lord it over them; and their great ones exercise authority upon them. But so shall it not be among you; but whosoever will be great among you, shall be your minister; and whosoever of you will be the chiefest, shall be servant of all. For even the Son of man came, not to be ministered unto but to minister, and to give his life a ransom for many. (Mark 10:42-45)

Every Christian, without exception, is called into the place where Jesus stood. To the extent that we are called to leadership, we are called to ministry, even costly ministry. The greater the leadership, the greater is to be the ministry. The word *minister* is not a title of power, but a designation of servanthood. There is to be no Christian guru. We must reject this constantly and carefully. A minister, a man who is a leader in the church of God (and never more needed than in a day like ours when the battle is so great), *must* make plain to the men, women, boys, and girls who come to places of leadership that instead of lording their authority over others and allowing it to become an ego trip, they are to serve in humility.

Again, Jesus said, "But be not ye called Rabbi; for one is your Master, even Christ, and all ye are brethren" (Matthew 23:8). This does not mean there is to be no order in the church. It does mean that the *basic* relationship between Christians is not that of elder and people, or pastor and people, but that of brothers and sisters in Christ. This denotes that there is one Father in the family and that his offspring are equal. There are different jobs to be done, different offices to be filled, but we as Christians are equal before one Master. We are not to seek a great title; we are to have the places together as brethren.

When Jesus said, "He that is greatest among you shall be your servant" (Matthew 23:11), He was not speaking in hyperbole or uttering a romantic idiom. Jesus Christ is the realist of all realists, and when He says this to us, He is telling us something specific we are to do.

Our attitude toward all men should be that of equality because we are common creatures. We are of one blood and kind. As I look across all the world, I must see every man as a fellow-creature, and I must be careful to have a sense of our equality on the basis of this common status. We must be careful in our thinking not to try to stand in the place of God to other men. We are fellow-creatures. And when I step from the creature-to-creature relationship into the brothers-and-sisters-in-Christ relationship within the church, how much more important to be a brother or sister to all who have the same Father. Orthodoxy, to be a Bible-believing Christian, always has two faces. It has a creedal face and a practicing face, and Christ emphasizes that that is to be the case here. Dead orthodoxy is always a contradiction in terms, and clearly that is so here; to be a Bible-believing Christian demands humility regarding others in the body of Christ.

Jesus gave us a tremendous example:

Jesus, knowing that the Father had given all things into his hands, and that he was come from God, and went to God; he riseth from supper, and laid aside his garments, and took a towel, and girded himself. After that he poureth water into a basin, and began to wash the disciples' feet, and to wipe them with the towel with which he was girded. . . . Ye call me Master and Lord; and ye say well; for so I am. If I, then, your Lord and Master, have washed your feet, ye also ought to wash one another's feet. For I have given you an example, that ye should do as I have done to you. Verily, verily, I say unto you, The servant is not greater than his lord; neither he that is sent greater than he that sent him. If ye know these things, happy are ye if ye do them. (John 13:3-5, 13-17)

Note that Jesus says that if we do these things, there will be happiness. It is not just knowing these things that brings happiness; it is doing them. Throughout Jesus' teaching these two words *know* and *do* occur constantly and always in that order. We cannot do until we know, but we can know without doing. The house built on the rock is the house of the man who knows and does. The house built on the sand is the house of the man who knows but does not do.

Christ washed the disciples' feet and dried them with the towel with which He was girded—that is, with his own clothing. He intended this to be a practical example of the mentality and action that should be seen in the midst of the people of God.

Taking the Lowest Place

Yet another statement of Jesus bears on our discussion:

And he put forth a parable to those who were bidden,
when he marked how they chose out the chief rooms;
saying unto them, When thou art bidden of any man to a
wedding, sit not down in the highest room; lest a more
honorable man than thou be bidden of him; and he that
bade thee and him come and say to thee, Give this man
place, and thou begin with shame to take the lowest room.
But when thou art bidden, go and sit down in the lowest
room that, when he that bade thee cometh, he may say
unto thee, Friend, go up higher; then shalt thou have
worship in the presence of them that sit at meat with
thee. For whosoever exalteth himself shall be abased; and
he that humbleth himself shall be exalted. (Luke 14:7-11)

Jesus commands Christians to seek consciously the lowest
room. All of us—pastors, teachers, professional religious workers
and nonprofessionals included—are tempted to say, "I will take
the larger place because it will give me more influence for Jesus
Christ." Both individual Christians and Christian organizations
fall prey to the temptation of rationalizing this way as we build
bigger and bigger empires. But according to the Scripture this is
backwards: we should consciously take the lowest place unless the
Lord Himself extrudes us into a greater one.

The word *extrude* is important here. To be extruded is to be
forced out under pressure into a desired shape. Picture a huge
press jamming soft metal at high pressure through a die, so that
the metal comes out in a certain shape. This is the way of the
Christian: he should choose the lesser place until God extrudes
him into a position of more responsibility and authority.

Let me suggest two reasons why we ought not grasp the larger
place. First, we should seek the lowest place because there it is
easier to be quiet before the face of the Lord. I did not say easy; in
no place, no matter how small or humble, is it easy to be quiet
before God. But it is certainly easier in some places than in
others. And the little places, where I can more easily be close to
God, should be my preference. I am not saying that it is impossible to be quiet before God in a greater place, but God must be
allowed to choose when a Christian is ready to be extruded into
such a place, for only He knows when a person will be able to
have some quietness before Him in the midst of increased pressure and responsibility.

Quietness and peace before God are more important than

any influence a position may seem to give, for we must stay in step with God to have the power of the Holy Spirit. If by taking a bigger place our quietness with God is lost, then to that extent our fellowship with Him is broken and we are living in the flesh, and the final result will not be as great, no matter how important the larger place may look in the eyes of other men or in our own eyes. Always there will be a battle, always we will be less than perfect, but if a place is too big and too active for our present spiritual condition, then it is too big.

We see this happen over and over again, and perhaps it has happened at some time to us: someone whom God has been using marvelously in a certain place takes it upon himself to move into a larger place and loses his quietness with God. Ten years later he may have a huge organization, but the power has gone, and he is no longer a real part of the battle in his generation. The final result of not being quiet before God is that less will be done, not more—no matter how much Christendom may be beating its drums or playing its trumpets for a particular activity.

So we must not go out beyond our depth. Take the smaller place so you have quietness before God. I am not talking about laziness; let me make that clear. That is something else, something too which God hates. I am not talking about copping out or dropping out. God's people are to be active, not seeking, on account of some false mystical concept, to sit constantly in the shade of a rock. There is no monasticism in Christianity. We will not be lazy in our relationship with God, because when the Holy Spirit burns, a man is consumed. We can expect to become physically tired in the midst of battle for our King and Lord; we should not expect all of life to be a vacation. We are talking about quietness before God as we are in His place for us. The size of the place is not important, but the consecration in that place is.

It must be noted that all these things which are true for an individual are true also for a group. A group can become activistic and take on responsibilities God has not laid upon it. For both the individual and the group, the first reason we are not to grasp (and the emphasis is on *grasp*) the larger place is that we must not lose our quietness with God.

The second reason why we should not seek the larger place is that if we deliberately and egotistically lay hold on leadership, wanting the drums to beat and the trumpets to blow, then we are not qualified for Christian leadership. Why? Because we have forgotten that we are brothers and sisters in Christ with other Christians. I have said on occasion that there is only one good kind of fighter for Jesus Christ—the man who does not like to fight. The belligerent man is never the one to be belligerent for Jesus. And it is exactly the same with leadership. The Christian leader should be a quiet man of God who is extruded by God's grace into some place of leadership.

We all have egoistic pressures inside us. We may have substantial victories over them and we may grow, but we never completely escape them in this life. The pressure is always there deep in my heart and soul, needing to be faced with honesty. These pressures are evident in the smallest of things as well as the greatest. I have seen fights over who was going to be the president of a Sunday school class composed of three members. The temptation has nothing to do with size. It comes from a spirit, a mentality, inside us. The person in leadership for leadership's sake is returning to the way of the world, like the boy dusting off the boss's chair and saying, "Someday I'll sit in it, and I'll make people jump."

One of the loveliest incidents in the early church occurred when Barnabas concluded that Paul was the man of the hour and then had to seek him out because Paul had gone back to Tarsus, his own little place. Paul was not up there nominating himself; he was back in Tarsus, even out of communication as far as we can tell. When Paul called himself "the chief of sinners, . . . not meet to be an apostle" (1 Timothy 1:15; 1 Corinthians 15:9), he was not speaking just for outward form's sake. From what he said elsewhere and from his actions we can see that this was Paul's mentality. Paul, the man of leadership for the whole Gentile world, was perfectly willing to be in Tarsus until God said to him, "This is the moment."

Being a Rod of God

The people who receive praise from the Lord Jesus will not in every case be the people who hold leadership in this life. There will be many persons who were sticks of wood that stayed close to God and were quiet before Him, and were used in power by Him in a place which looks small to men.

Each Christian is to be a rod of God in the place of God for him. We must remember throughout our lives that in God's sight there are no little people and no little places. Only one thing is important: to be consecrated persons in God's place for us, at each moment. Those who think of themselves as little people in little places, if committed to Christ and living under His Lordship in the whole of life, may, by God's grace, change the flow of our generation. And as we get on a bit in our lives, knowing how weak we are, if we look back and see we have been somewhat used of God, then we should be the rod "surprised by joy."

Acknowledgments

"The Waning Authority of Christ in the Churches" by A. W. Tozer; used by permission of Christian Publications. (Available as a tract through Christian Publications, 3825 Hartzdale Drive, Camp Hill, PA 17011.)

"What Will the Lord Say to Us All When He Returns?" by William Culbertson; used by permission of Moody Bible Institute, 820 N. LaSalle Street, Chicago, IL 60610.

"If Good Men Will Not . . ." by V. Raymond Edman; used by permission of Wheaton College, Wheaton, IL 60187.

"The Christian Message to the World" by D. Martyn Lloyd-Jones; used by permission of Mrs. Lloyd-Jones and taken from the book *God's Way of Reconciliation*, Chapter 6, under the title "But God," published by Banner of Truth, The Grey House, 3 Murrayfield Rd., Edinburgh, Scotland.

"The Eternal Security of the Believer" by Henry Allan Ironside; used by permission of Loizeau Brothers, 1238 Corlies Avenue, Neptune, NJ 07753.

"Your Right to Heaven" by Donald Grey Barnhouse; used by permission of Tenth Presbyterian Church, Seventeenth and Spruce Streets, Philadelphia, PA 19103.

"The Birthday of Souls" by James McGinlay; used by permission of William B. Eerdmans, 255 Jefferson Avenue S.E., Grand Rapids, MI 49503.

"When God's Patience Wears Out" by John R. Rice; used by permission of Sword of the Lord Foundation, P.O. Box 1099, Murfreesboro, TN 37133.

"Payday Someday" by Robert G. Lee. Copyright 1957, 1985 by Zondervan Publishing House, Grand Rapids, MI 49506. Used by permission.